AT THE
DEAD HOURS
OF MIDNIGHT

AT THE
DEAD HOURS
OF MIDNIGHT

A BLOODY REIGN OF TERROR
IN THE GREAT SMOKY MOUNTAINS

RICHARD WAY

STANFORD JOHNSON

PREVIOUSLY PUBLISHED AS "*THE EYES OF MIDNIGHT*"

Cover image edit by Mike Duvall

Manuscript format assistance by Lorna Keathley

ISBN – 979-8-218-10694-2

In honor of two genuine Sevier County heroes
Thomas Houston Davis and John Sam Springs

"The only thing necessary for the triumph of evil
is for good men to do nothing."
—origin of quote unknown

"The time has come when some man must undertake it,
or our county is ruined."
—Sevier County Deputy Sheriff Thomas Houston Davis

CONTENTS

Epilogue

Acknowledgements

Appendix—Timeline of Significant Whitecapping Events

Index

About the Authors

PREFACE

A union musician in Knoxville during his teen years, Richard Way played drums on the Cas Walker Hour. When Cas wasn't performing, he and Richard would sit on a rolled up canvas, and Cas captivated Richard's imagination with wild tales about the goings on in Sevier County in the 1890s between the White Caps and Blue Bills. Those stories ruminated for decades, until Richard commissioned Robert Wilson to write *The Eyes of Midnight: A Time of Terror in East Tennessee*, which was published in 2016.

Stanford Johnson's connection to the White Caps of Sevier County saga is of the same ilk as those who wish it would just go away. His maternal grandmother's maternal grandmother was Nancy Teletha Wynn Yearout, eldest daughter of Elkanah Mitchell Wynn and oldest sister of Pleasant D. Wynn. Stan first learned about Pleas Wynn and his infamy around 2000, while doing genealogy research to establish his qualifications for membership in First Families of Tennessee.

Nearly two decades after Stan qualified for First Families of Tennessee, he met Richard. Richard felt *The Eyes of Midnight* had not gained the audience it merited, and eventually asked Stan if he'd be interested in working on a second edition. Because of his family connection to the story, Stan was excited to take on this project.

We made many wholesale changes in our attempt to give the reader a fuller experience: we changed the title and the cover, and devoted chapters to an introductory chapter on Whitecapping, and chapters dedicated to John Sam Springs and Thomas Houston Davis, and a couple of chapters to explain how and why the White Caps transitioned from an extralegal vigilante organization whose purpose was to "uphold Victorian morals," to a marauding gang of "toughs," or Brood of Vipers and Den of Thieves. Another gem we mined were actual trial transcripts from the November 1897 Tipton/Wynn murder case we found in the Donald F. Paine Collection in the Special

Collections Department at The University of Tennessee's Hodges Library.

Because the White Caps in Sevier County originally called themselves the "White Caps of Emert's Cove,"[1] and because John Sam Springs basically said, "not in my back yard," we think it's highly plausible John Sam Springs was the founder of the Blue Bills. Whitecapping ended in Emert's Cove not long after it began, then seemed to metastasize and take root in the other civil districts which made up Sevier County.

There is no evidence or reports of any Whitecapping incidents in Emert's Cove after 1892. One incident that occurred in September 1894 reportedly took place in Gatlinburg, even though the intended target, U. S. Congressman John C. Houk passed through Emert's Cove on his way from Jones Cove to Gatlinburg.[2] This suggests that Springs' presence was formidable, and seems to have been a deterrent to Whitecapping in Emert's Cove from the time he run them out of his community.

We added more photographs of some of the key people. As far as we have been able to verify, the photographs of Laura McMahan Whaley and her sister, Elizabeth "Lizzie" McMahan Chandler, have never before been published. But if you've seen the sketches of those two ladies in the Crozier book and Cas Walker's book, it is apparent the sketches were made from these two original photographs.

We feel one of the most significant improvements is the addition of newspaper articles. Newspaper articles have made it possible to more closely date-stamp some of the events. Because these stories were often transmitted by word of mouth and delivered on horseback,

---

[1] WHITE CAPS IN SEVIER, *Knoxville Daily Tribune*, January 27, 1892
[2] WET WITH BLOOD, *The Republican Leader*, Knoxville, Tennessee, September 27, 1894

it was helpful to follow the storylines from newspaper edition to newspaper edition.

A prime example of date-stamping an event is the genesis of the Blue Bills, that counter-vigilante group "organized to resist the White Caps."[3] It has been previously reported that Dr. James A. Henderson founded the Blue Bills after Mary Breeden died in August 1893, from the wounds the White Caps inflicted on her in May 1893. The newspaper article from May 1892 reports the Blue Bills were organized for the aforementioned reason. It does not stand to reason that Dr. Henderson founded the Blue Bills in 1893, if a newspaper article reported their existence more than a year earlier. This does not diminish in any way Dr. Henderson's contribution to the saga, as he was instrumental in eradicating Whitecapping in Sevier County through his leadership and financial support.

Newspaper articles also make the stories come alive in a different, real-time sort of way, as these stories were being lived out and reported on. And the language of the day! We're certain you will enjoy the language the writers employed to tell the stories. Sometimes the language is graphic and sometimes it's rather humorous, but their words give you a snapshot into the syntax and vernacular of the time.

William Joseph Cummings III published a Master's thesis in 1988, as part of his Master of Arts degree at the University of Tennessee titled, *Community, Violence, and the Nature of Change: Whitecapping in Sevier County, Tennessee, During the 1890's.*[4] We don't want to overstate the significance of this document, but Cummings makes assertions in his thesis that change the very nature of Whitecapping in Sevier County, from initially enforcing community standards of conduct and behavior to something far more nefarious.

---

[3] WHITE CAPS AGAIN, *Knoxville Tribune*, May 18, 1892
[4] Cummings, William Joseph, "Community, Violence, and the Nature of Change: Whitecapping in Sevier County, Tennessee, During the 1890's." Master's Thesis, University of Tennessee, 1988

Cummings seems to attribute the authorship of the Crozier book to Sheriff Tom Davis, although others who've referenced the Crozier book credit Crozier himself as likely being the author.

Our goal from the outset has been to produce the definitive account of Whitecapping in Sevier County, but for obvious reasons there are still holes in the story, and always will be. That which was taken to the graves by all the participants in the saga would most certainly fill many volumes, and even then there would be gaps and inconsistencies in the story.

We hope you enjoy our book, and that you feel your understanding of Whitecapping in Sevier County has grown exponentially. If you hadn't previously heard of the White Caps, then we hope your experience with this work was enlightening.

History must be studied and the lessons applied going forward, else they are subject to be repeated, and this type of degenerate conduct should not be condoned, then be repeated and tolerated.

Richard and Stan

INTRODUCTION

You may or may not have heard about the White Caps of Sevier County. If you have heard of them and think you know the story—think again. If you haven't heard of them, fasten your seatbelts, because you're about to hear a story as true as we know how to tell it. Whitecapping in Sevier County was a movement that began as a vigilante response to community deviance, but was rather quickly hijacked by prominent Sevier Countians as an illegal and illegitimate means to gain and maintain power.

There have been a number of books devoted to telling the story of Whitecapping in Sevier County, but what if I told you the previously published accounts have been cover stories, perpetuated to hide even more reprehensible truths?

"Shortly, after the *charivari* of the prostitutes in Emert's Cove, *whitecap gangs were organized by justices of the peace* who were able to protect their men by dismissing the whitecap cases in their court for lack of evidence. On the few cases that were bound over to the circuit court, the justices were still able to intercede for the night riders by selecting fellow whitecaps to serve on grand and petit juries. As whitecapping grew in popularity, the night riders were able to protect themselves further from grand and petit juries by intimidating state witnesses. Thus the "vigilantes" were able to subvert the traditional balance between legal and extra-legal justice. Soon merchants and mechanics joined the organization in order to attract business; and whitecaps began to take on the trappings of a mystic fraternal organization, like the Masons or Oddfellows, complete with secret meetings and signs, blood oaths, and ritual garb. Eventually, the justices and other local politicians identified themselves with the vigilantes at election time and sought their vote.

"Within a short time, whitecap gangs were being sponsored by wealthy farmers who helped the vigilantes by guaranteeing their bail and providing counsel during court proceedings. It is said that no whitecap ever languished in jail or ever skipped on his bond. Like the early vigilantes who were unsatisfied with a slow and ineffective court system, the landowners saw in the whitecaps an opportunity to expedite their potential legal problems with troublesome tenants."[5]

The most obvious, and also the most despicable, example of landowners using Whitecapping methods to deal with "troublesome tenants" was the murder for hire of William and Laura Whaley, commissioned by William Robert "Bob" Catlett, one of the wealthiest landowners in Sevier County in the 1890s. Even though Catlett escaped the gallows himself, it was almost universally believed by Sevier Countians that he was guilty of contracting that heinous act. He hired James Catlett Tipton and Pleasant D. Wynn to kill the Whaleys, because the Whaleys had testified against him and Robert "Bob" Wade in a case where Catlett and Wade used Whitecapping methods to deal with a troublesome tenant, Walter Maples.

When you consider the totality of the story, it is obvious that the landowners and Justices of the Peace colluded in order to gain an economic advantage over others. Call it what you will—collusion or organized crime—the Whitecapping saga was, to quote Thomas Hobbes, "nasty, brutish and short."

col·lude /kəˈloōd/ cooperate in a secret or unlawful way in order to gain an advantage over others

---

[5] Cummings, 19-20

You may have never heard the term "charivari." "Charivari" or "Rough music," was the term for a European and North American custom, where a mock parade was assembled in a community, accompanied by a discordant mock serenade. The crowd purposed to make as much noise as possible, to draw attention to perceived or real wrongdoers. Villages used charivari in cases where marriages were disapproved, adulterous relationships, against wife beaters and unmarried mothers. The charivari or rough music mutated into extralegal means used by communities to correct real or perceived breaches or violations of community norms.

Industrialization had not made it to Sevier County's backcountry, but the world's oldest profession had. The morals charge on which the convictions against prostitutes were being sought was lewdness, which in that era comprised fornication and adultery.

So, while charivari was the original motivation for the inception of Whitecapping in Sevier county, as you'll see, it very quickly devolved into something far more nefarious.

Cummings says that in Sevier County, Justices of the Peace (sometimes referred to by their honorific title "Squire"), not only organized White Cap gangs but subverted justice "by dismissing whitecap cases in their court for lack of evidence."[6] He goes on to say that, "Within a short time, whitecap gangs were being sponsored by wealthy farmers who helped vigilantes by guaranteeing their bail and providing counsel during court proceedings."

It was also reported that White Cap methods were used in order to frighten off landowners, so others could purchase their land "at a song."[7] When presented with this information, a retired Methodist preacher in Blount County said, "That explains why my grandfather moved to Blount

[6] Cummings, 19
[7] WHITE CAPS AGAIN, *Knoxville Sentinel*, February 20, 1897

County from Sevier County—he always said he couldn't buy any land in Sevier County."

What makes this particularly fascinating, is his grandfather was from one of those prominent families with strong ties to Whitecapping, but probably on the right side of law and order. It has been our theory that just as the Civil War divided families in the 1860s, Whitecapping more than likely divided some Sevier County families in the 1890s.

And we know Whitecapping destroyed other families. Captain Elkanah Mitchell "E. M." Wynn, another prominent Sevier Countian, lost two sons, William and Pleas, because of their involvement with the White Caps.

As you'll see, William "Bill" Wynn, E. M. Wynn's second oldest son and a Justice of the Peace, was very influential in the White Caps organization, and was suspected of being "the real leader of that organization."[8] On the occasion of Bill Wynn's death, Deputy Sheriff Tom Davis went as far as to say, *"I do not think there will be any more whitecapping in our county. Squire Bill Wynn was the bully of Sevierville and has been until his death for the past ten years."*

Could Squire Bill Wynn have been the "High Cockalorum" or "Chief Mogul" we'll read about later?

One recorded example of the rampant mockeries of justice by Justices of the Peace is evidenced by William Wynn hearing a case against his younger brother Pleas Wynn. "She swore out a warrant against Wynne (Pleas), but he was tried before his brother, William Wynne, who is a justice of the peace, and was discharged."[9] This was after Pleas was implicated in the Whaley killings, for which he was one of the two men hanged on July 5, 1899.

The aforementioned collusion and illegitimacy of the Justice of the Peace/County Court system, and the use of threats and violence against

---

[8] SAFE IN KNOX COUNTY JAIL, *The Knoxville Tribune*, April 13, 1898
[9] SEVIER IS QUIET, *The Knoxville Tribune*, March 20, 1897

Sevier Countians amounted to organized crime, and this leaves us with a number of questions.

What was the true motivation for the proliferation of Whitecapping in Sevier County, if the estimates are correct and there were between 650-1500 White Caps conducting more than a dozen White Cap raids a night as E. W. Crozier suggests?

> "In the write-up of the White-caps and their depredations in Sevier County, it has not been the purpose of the writer to give full and detailed accounts of all the minor offenses committed by them.
>
> "It would take a volume of more than one thousand pages to give such accounts, and do the subject justice, there frequently occurring more than a dozen whippings in a single night."[10]

And if there were that many White Caps conducting that many raids, why were only a handful charged and convicted of their crimes?

Is it possible that "the powers that be" were relieved that only two would pay the ultimate penalty for the sins of so many, so that the Whitecapping stain would just go away? If that is true, a whole lot of people got away with a whole lot of crimes.

We ask that you consider these questions as you read *At the Dead Hours of Midnight: A Bloody Reign of Terror in the Great Smoky Mountains*, and we thank you for reading our book.

Richard and Stan

---

[10] E. W. Crozier, *The White Caps: A History of the Organization in Sevier County* (1899), 180

1

Two Bad Men are Hanged,
But Were They Scapegoats?

July 5, 1899, like December 28, 1896, is a date that will live in infamy in Sevier County, Tennessee. James Catlett Tipton and Pleasant D. Wynn were hanged by their necks until declared dead, on a gallows inside an enclosure built for that purpose in Sevierville, Tennessee. The event made headlines in newspapers all across the Land of the Free and Home of the Brave—Marion, OH, Birmingham, AL, Washington, D.C., Pittsburgh, PA, Iowa City, IA, Kansas City, MO, Sacramento, CA, to name but a few.

A common theme among the newspaper articles was the idea that their executions ended the reign of terror, which is debatable, as some consider the crime for which they were hanged the end of the reign of terror. We personally believe that *if the saga ever truly ended at all*, it did so with the final acquittal of William Robert Catlett in 1904.

Sheriff Tom Davis and a handful of others were crowded onto a wooden platform that creaked beneath its load as the scene played out. Joining Sheriff Davis, Tipton and Wynn on the scaffold were Mrs. Wynn, Mrs. Tipton, Rev. M. A. Rule, Rev. W. W. Pyott, Jailer J. F. Springer,

Deputy Sheriff John Sam Springs, Deputy Sheriff Keener and Deputy Sheriff Hugh Nicely.

A cluster of doctors, Dr. Zachary David "Z. D." Massey, Dr. G. E. Sharp, Dr. G. C. Ellis, and Dr. E. H. Pierce, stood beneath the scaffold to examine the bodies and declare them dead after their hearts beat their last beats.[11]

Seven years of beatings and bullets, fear and treachery, unspeakable cruelty inflicted by neighbor upon neighbor. And this was the result—more death.

The difference this time was these two men needed to die. Almost no one in the crowd would dispute that. Maybe what these men did God could forgive, but the State of Tennessee and the good people of Sevier County, Tennessee, could not. Or maybe the gallows served as a sacrificial altar, upon which two men died, for which others thankfully believed their roles in Sevier County Whitecapping would forever be dismissed.

Tipton and Wynn, two of Sheriff Davis's old Eureka baseball teammates, stood a few steps away from Davis talking in hushed voices to their wives and ministers. Davis had been a captain of the Eureka baseball team in their youth.[12]

Fervent prayers for forgiveness rose through the cloudy gloom to a God with more mercy—it was hoped—than these two had themselves demonstrated. Wynn and Tipton were strikingly calm. Occasionally they glanced at the ropes, carefully knotted with nooses at one end and Judgment at the other. And they talked in whispers with their women, who would shortly be widowed as a consequence of their husbands' crimes.

At the court's instruction, the gallows had been enclosed inside a high, stockade-like fence to provide some level of privacy to a legal proceeding

---

[11] W. P. Chandler, PLEAS WYNN AND CATLETT TIPTON'S SPIRITS DISPATCHED TO ETERNITY, *The Knoxville Weekly Sentinel*, Knoxville, Tennessee, July 5, 1899
[12] Crozier, 146, 149

that would prove to be the last of its kind in Sevier County. In a macabre irony, James Catlett Tipton who was a carpenter by trade, had assisted with the construction of the very structure behind which his death sentence would be carried out.[13]

Ninety-six people were allowed inside the enclosure, most of them family members, law enforcers, clergymen, doctors, lawyers and newspapermen. It was crowded, and it was hot, made all the more uncomfortable by Victorian-era fashions that dictated proper women be covered from neck to shoe top and men wear string ties, heavy coats and trousers—no matter the temperature.

Outside the fence, the largest crowd ever assembled in Sevierville at the time—about three thousand people—milled about the courthouse square, their presence and numbers a testament to the significance of this event.[14]

Tipton and Wynn were asked if they had anything to say, and they both replied that they committed their final statements to writing, and had furnished them to a newspaper reporter for publication.[15]

Catlett Tipton's Story.

"My story on the witness stand, about the crime, is a true story. Bob Catlett is the cause of my having to die today. He just kept after me, until he overpowered me, and now I must say farewell to earth. Let my fate be a lesson to all who are tempted to keep the company of evil doers. It seems hard for me to part from my dear wife and little children, but I feel that I am going home to a happy, peaceful abode, where there are no

---

[13] BLOOD WILL HAVE BLOOD, *The Journal and Tribune*, Knoxville, Tennessee, July 6, 1899
[14] Ibid
[15] Ibid

temptations to sin. Let my evil deeds be forgotten. If I ever did any good, I hope it will be remembered.

"I hope it may never be the fate of anyone here to suffer the penalty I am now about to suffer, at the hands of a man, who caused my conviction on untrue evidence. May God in heaven forgive him, as I have done. He sought the reward, more than he did the perpetrators of the crime.

"I hope he will never cause another man to be convicted upon false testimony. I know that when Jett Jenkins swore that Pleas Wynn came to his house, and got a pistol and some whiskey, on the night of the Whaley murder, he swore falsely and without any foundation.

"And when James Gass swore that I told him I was into the killing, and that I had to prove myself out, he swore falsely. I FEEL THAT I SHOULD SAY WE ARE GUILTY AS CHARGED, but we were convicted on perjured testimony from beginning to end.

"I would not care to die so much if the third party was only to go the same way. I know there is no evidence against him except ours. It will not be long now until he, Robert Catlett, will give himself up to the officers. And the result will be an acquittal. But I shall not clamor at all.

"I do not want my friends to grieve for me. I think sweet peace is my future, and with a last farewell to all, I close to permit Sheriff Davis to perform the duty which it seems, to him, will be pleasant."

(Signed)   J. CATLETT TIPTON.

It is fascinatingly candid to us that Tipton readily admits his guilt, but says they were "convicted on perjured testimony." The fact that Pleas

Wynn goes on to say the same thing is not surprising, since the two men shared a Knox County jail cell for many months leading up to their trials and eventual execution. Tipton also suggests that Catlett, who had escaped recapture following an acquittal in May 1899, was waiting for his and Wynn's death sentences to be carried out.

Pleas. Wynn's Story.

"I am soon to die, and, before the fatal moment arrives, permit me to say that I have no murmer (sic) against justice, although I was convicted on the testimony of perjured witnesses, who falsely swore my life away.

"Being guilty, I feel that I should tell all about it, and but for my attorney, I would have done it long before I did. I know that my conviction, on the evidence, was a mockery of justice, but I know further that the moral turpitude of my crime was such as to merit the very severe punishment, although I did not commit the crime of killing the Whaleys.

"Bob Catlett deserves punishment that he may never receive. I hope he will not lead anyone else into trouble. I hope too that the God of mercy will forgive him for his past life.

"As to my conviction for the Whaley murders I would be glad to have my testimony emphasized by saying that I told the whole truth.

"I regret that I have brought any trouble on the families to which I belong, and whose name I bear. I would say to every man to keep good company or none. Be industrious and sober and a life of peace will result. I believe truly that God's eternal word should be the guiding star of our lives, and it is the sheet anchor of my soul today.

"I do not want my friends to grieve for me. I think that sweet peace is my future. I bid everyone good bye and will close to allow Sheriff Davis to perform the duty which it seems will be a pleasant one for him."

(Signed)   P. D. WYNN

At 1:02 PM on July 5, 1899, Sheriff Davis nodded to Deputy Sheriff Keener, and Keener pulled the lever releasing the trapdoor. Tipton and Wynn dropped to their deaths.

To quote Paul Harvey, a man whose voice and stories Americans loved listening to on the radio for generations:

"And now, the rest of the story."

2

The Roots of Whitecapping

Whitecapping's roots were in the Midwest, particularly in Indiana, decades before it appeared in Tennessee. It started out in some rural communities in the United States, primarily in the mid to late 1800s, as an entirely illegal vigilante enforcement mechanism to police community behavior standards, without having to adhere to the lawfulness of due process.

While they were in the loosest sense an organization, there were never any official rolls, which made it all the more difficult to identify, charge, prosecute and convict them when they committed their crimes.

Typically, White Caps would disguise themselves with a full-body covering of white fabric with holes cut for the eyes. Though the description may summon images of the Ku Klux Klan, White Caps did not wear the conical—and comical—headdress of the Klan. And the White Caps were motivated more by morality than by ethnicity, though some White Capping activity did target ethnic groups. The historical record suggests that race was never a factor in Sevier County Whitecapping.

Whitecapping eventually became institutionalized by formal law, and the application of its legal definition became more general than the specific movement itself. The following is an example of a state statute (Mississippi) on Whitecapping:

> "Any person or persons who shall, by placards, or other writing, or verbally, attempt by threats, direct or implied, of injury to the person or property of another, to intimidate such other person into an abandonment or change of home or employment, shall, upon conviction, be fined not exceeding five hundred dollars, or imprisoned in the county jail not exceeding six months, or in the penitentiary not exceeding five years, as the court, in its discretion may determine."[16]

Over time, these vigilante groups became known by a variety of names—Whitecaps, Regulators, Night Riders, Bald Knobbers and Ku Kluxers.

A significant element of the perceived need to implement extralegal enforcement of community standards was a condition called "community consensus." Vigilante solutions to problems the legal system was unable or unwilling to correct seemed a natural expression of community consensus. This accounts for the perceived acceptance of the Sevier County White Caps' use of violence to impose the community's standards of behavior and conduct upon the wayward women who set up shop in the Emert's Cove/Copeland Creek communities in Sevier County before January 1892.[17]

The sort of tacit approval on the part of some Sevier Countians evidently inspired others, in other civil districts to incorporate

---

[16] 2013 Mississippi Code, Title 97 – CRIMES, Chapter 3 – CRIMES AGAINST THE PERSON, 97-3-87 – Threats and intimidation; whitecapping
[17] WHITE CAPS IN SEVIER, *Knoxville Daily Tribune*, January 27, 1892

Whitecapping methods, but as a means to a different end. The motivation for Whitecapping in the other civil districts very quickly changed from the enforcement of Victorian morals to a lawless organization constructed to protect lawbreakers of all types from prosecution. And, as Cas Walker points out in his book,[18]

> "Crime and wrongdoing is always progressive, and will increase in its influence in proportion to the encouragement it receives. Whenever it becomes popular in any community to violate the law, it is not necessary to stop to discuss whether or not crimes will be committed in that community. It follows as a natural consequence."

The May 1892 article in the Knoxville Tribune accurately and tragically predicted the course Whitecapping in Sevier County would ultimately take, and adequately described the mood of Sevier Countians at the beginning of the White Caps saga.[19]

> "Everybody is afraid to do anything toward having the outlaws brought to justice, for fear of suffering at their hands but it is whispered that the leader of the gang is a Justice of the peace. Over five hundred revolvers have been sold throughout the county within the last two months, the purchasers being citizens of the highest standing, who fear that they may unwittingly incur the displeasure of the white caps, and be visited by them and if such happens to be the case, they want to be prepared for the occasion.
>
> "A wholesale killing is looked for at any time for the people are becoming aroused, the officers have thus far done nothing to

---

[18] Orton Caswell "Cas" Walker, *The Whitecaps of Sevier County* (1937), 32
[19] WHITE CAPS AGAIN, *Knoxville Tribune*, May 18, 1892

stop the outrages, and the people are determined to see what they can do."

There's a lot going on in this portion of the article that is worthy of note, and worthy of unpacking.

Notice the climate in Sevier County, and the fact that "everybody is afraid to do anything." This suggests that from the outset the saga quite naturally and predictably evolved into a reign of terror. Five hundred revolvers sold in two months, in a county with a population of about 20,000, seems to support the belief that the fear of potential violence was tangible, and for good reason.

It is particularly fascinating that, as early as May 1892, a Justice of the Peace was believed to be "the leader of the gang."

And the last nugget mined from this article, "officers have thus far done nothing to stop the outrages," suggests an unwillingness on the part of law enforcement to protect and serve those whom they were elected and appointed to protect and serve. Might it have been because they, too, had already been infiltrated by the White Caps?

George DeLozier was the High Sheriff of Sevier County when the White Cap infestation began, and his predecessor was Captain Elkanah Mitchell "E. M." Wynn. It has been suggested that DeLozier didn't go after the White Caps vigorously, and as previously mentioned, two of Captain Wynn's sons became casualties in the unfolding saga.

In 1894, republican Millard Fillmore Maples ran for sheriff against DeLozier and Wynn,[20] and promised to appoint a democrat as a deputy sheriff if elected. Thomas Houston Davis was that democrat, and maybe because he had been an outspoken critic of Whitecapping in Sevier County. As you'll see in subsequent chapters, the union between Maples and Davis was consequential in the eradication of Whitecapping in Sevier County.

---

[20] Crozier, 165

While the true identity of the White Caps were known only by the members of that mystic order, in a county with about 4,000 registered all-male voters, allegiances would have generally been known. Cas Walker, whose own father was a Blue Bill, believed that was the case.

> "While no one but the White-caps themselves knew absolutely who belonged to the clan, yet nearly everyone had a general idea who they were and when a whipping occurred some particular person or persons were usually suspected of doing it.[21]"

It has been suggested that another motivation for conducting Whitecap raids was the settling of old scores—or feuding here in the mountains. And it makes perfect sense that anytime the White Caps conducted a raid for any reason other than upholding Victorian morals, the object of the raid would have suspected who his or her enemies in the community were, and quite likely had an idea of who had committed the crime.

[22]

WHITE CAPS IN SEVIER

Make Living Uncomfortable for the Wicked.

A band of men calling themselves the "White Caps of Emert's Cove," in Sevier county, are making it uncomfortable for all who are at heart inclined to be wicked.

They have been organized about six weeks and have whipped a number of women of lewd proclivities.

The other night they attempted to raid a house of ill repute, but the inmates were prepared and opened upon them with Winchesters, causing them to beat a retreat.

---

[21] Walker, 22

[22] The first newspaper article seems to suggest the White Caps organized in Sevier County some time in 1891. It is also important to note they called themselves "The White Caps of Emert's Cove." WHITE CAPS IN SEVIER, January 27, 1892

23

White Caps in Sevier County.

KNOXVILLE, TENN., Jan. 27.—Last Monday a band of men calling themselves "White Caps of Emert's Cove," attempted to raid a house of ill repute in Sevier County, Tennessee, but were repulsed by the inmates, who opened fire on the midnight visitors with Winchesters.

---

[23] A portion of the same article a day later. Chattanooga Daily Times, White Caps in Sevier County, *Chattanooga Daily Times*, Chattanooga, Tennessee, Thursday, January 28, 1892

3

Origins of Sevier County Whitecapping [24]

Sevier County had a population of 22,021 in 1900, up from 18,761 in the 1890 census,[25] and had been a place where people mostly kept to themselves, taking care of their own business and letting others take care of theirs. In the northern and western parts of the county, the long Tennessee summers allowed landowners to grow what they needed for commerce—wheat, corn and vegetables, or hay for the livestock—which resulted in a number of wealthy, prominent landowners.

In the eastern and southern sections forested mountains rose above the flatlands. The folds and hollows of the hills were home to only the most hardy—those who were content with only minimal contact with others. There they hunted the woods, made their home-brew whiskey and scratched a hardscrabble existence out of a terrain generally not suited for agriculture. The sun's morning arrival came a little later here, because it had to rise over The Great Smoky Mountains, first permeating the deep forest, then shedding abundant sunlight on the fertile river bottoms.

---

[24] WHITE CAPS IN SEVIER, January 27, 1892
[25] U.S. Decennial Census 1790-1960

13

Until the early 1890s, the serenity of this county was most often broken only by the church bells on Sunday morning. Neighbors, if you had any, supported each other with a hot meal or a load of firewood for a shut-in down the road. When necessary, they helped each other dig a well or a grave.

It has been suggested in previous accounts of Whitecapping in Sevier County, we believe erroneously, that newspaper articles in Knoxville newspapers reporting Whitecapping incidents in Indiana were the inspiration for Whitecapping in Sevier County. Whitecapping may have begun in Indiana around 1837, but there were reported incidents of Whitecapping in and around east Tennessee around the same time it manifested in Sevier County. [26]

KNOXVILLE WHITECAPS.

This Organization Has at Last Secured a Foothold in Our Midst.

The following suggestive letter from the Whitecap headquarters for Knoxville and vicinity has been received by the SENTINEL and is given the publicity it seems to deserve. Their stationery is duly stamped with the Whitecap seal, which is a white helmet in a black background. Any of our readers receiving a visit from the agents of this company will confer a favor by mentioning to them that they saw their advertisement in this paper. Following is the letter:

"WHITE-CAP" HEADQUARTERS
FOR KNOXVILLE AND VICIN-
ITY, March 16, 1891.

Editor Sentinel.

As you will see, by above heading, we expect to carry on operations in this ocality, as we are confident that such work is needed here. We don't confine our operati n to married men only, f r we make the you g man our specialty; but will not overlook the married man. We have long looked upon th s part of your State as being a good field for this kind of work, and shall begin operations at once, and would suggest that you give notice of our appearance, in order to let all escape who will take heed. We are

PETE NINEY, Grand Regulator,
BILL SHUMP, Vice-Regulator,
I. K. SATORLLY, 2d Vice-Regulator.

Surely reports of Whitecaps organizing in "Knoxville and vicinity" would have been far more influential regionally than reports of Whitecapping in some place as distant as Indiana.

---

[26] KNOXVILLE WHTECAPS, *The Evening Sentinel*, March 17, 1891

[27]

WEDDING ENDS IN MURDER.

Mountain Moonshine Gets a Neighborhood Into Trouble.

The following special from Ducktown gives the particulars of a tragic event near the North Carolina line.

A very bloodthirsty and revolting battle and crime took place in this section this evening about 9 o'clock, at Wolf Creek, a short distance from here.

A wild and unruly mob had assembled at the house of one Bell. Whisky flowed like water, and apparently all were chuck full and ready for a fight or frolic.

The substance of the above meeting is that: Old man Bell, the great-granddaddy of the next generation, is a very old gentleman and a man of considerable means. A few weeks ago his wife suddenly died and the old man was almost crazy. However, all his people strenuously objected to his taking another helpmeet, but still the old man thought he knew best. Therefore, he took unto himself a girl about seventeen years of age, and together they went to occupy the old homestead. This incensed his children so that they decided to see what there was in white cap methods, and after the bride had been ushered into the happy and contented home the devil seemed to get into the whole layout.

No demonstration was made, however, until the crowd began to feel good from the effects of mountain moonshine and then everybody began to feel like fighting. Better counsel prevailed for awhile till the women also began to drink freely of bugjuice. Then they decided on action—and immediate action at that. The women of the Bell household disguised themselves and politely requested wife No. 2 to accompany them outside. There they stripped her to the waist, tied her to a tree and proceeded to administer about 100 lashes, almost killing her.

Among the spectators was one John Ballew, who witnessed the whole performance. After the whipping next day, Ballew was brought up as a witness against the women white caps and swore that he saw the whole affair, and the justice committed them.

This made the Bell gang mad, and the result was that they visited Ballew's house, intending to give him a round thrashing, but they failed. Mr. Ballew had a Winchester, and when called to his door and informed of the object of their midnight visit he emptied the contents of his rifle into the crowd, killing John Bell and fatally wounding six or eight others. They did not expect this kind of a reception and consequently took to their heels and fled for their lives.

Intense excitement prevails in Ducktown and vicinity, and it is expected that more bloodshed will follow. At present everything is quiet. The parties connected with this affair are all good people and this accident is greatly to be deplored.

While the phrase "white cap methods" was used to describe the events before they took place, perhaps someone somewhere else interpreted this as a way to go about criminal behavior while not actually being a sworn member of the White Cap organization. It is also particularly noteworthy that "The women of the Bell household" were the ones who "disguised themselves," which may have been the inspiration for women to participate in the original Whitecapping incident in Emert's Cove:[28]

"The white cap movement originated in Emmert's cove two or three months ago, and was headed by two men and a number

---

[27] WEDDING ENDS IN MURDER, *The Evening Sentinel*, May 8, 1891
[28] WHITE CAPS AGAIN, *Knoxville Tribune*, May 18, 1892

of married women who sought to take revenge upon men who had proved false to their wedding vows."

And as you'll learn in subsequent chapters, the Sevier County White Caps grew exponentially in number, as thugs and cowards joined the organization *after they committed their crimes*, so that they, too, could be afforded the legal protection provided by that mystic order.

TENNESSEE WHITE CAPS

Flay a Man For Alleged Ill-Treatment of His Wife.

By Associated Press.

NASHVILLE, July 16.—A Tullahoma, Tenn., special says: There was a White Cap outrage committed here last night. It was done so quietly and by unmasked parties so that it is next to impossible to get any authentic particulars. Masked men seized Ed O'Connor, of this place, and took him to a grove in the suburbs of town where they whipped him severely with switches. The alleged cause is that he mistreated his wife.

The Tullahoma White Caps incident seemingly represented a more traditional extralegal response to enforcement of community consensus.[29]

TREATS IT SERIOUSLY.

An Editor Who Received a Notice from the White Caps.

A newspaper man in trouble. Mr. George H. Freeman, editor of the Harriman Advance, several days ago received notice that other climes would be more congenial to him and his absence more acceptable to "White Caps."

Mr. Freeman was in the city yesterday to consult with Hon. H. B. Lindsay in regard to the matter.

He stated that on the 17th of this month he received a notice from parties writing over the signature of "White Caps" that if he was not out of Harriman by the 27th of August, he would be tarred and feathered and set on fire, etc.

Mr. Freeman treats the matter seriously and is seeking legal advice in the matter, although it is probable some one is "doing" him for fun.

He suspects certain parties of having sent the communication and may prosecute them. At the head of the communication was the customary skull and cross bones. The warning expires by limitation tomorrow. It is not known whether Mr. Freeman will venture back or not.

It seems that the gentleman, in the course of his journalistic career at Harriman, has seen fit to make some attacks upon parties bringing liquor into the sanctified precincts of Harriman. This may or may not have resulted in his receipt of the delicate little missive.

And as evidenced by the Harriman incident, Whitecapping continued to evolve in East Tennessee from an extralegal means of enforcing community consensus to nothing more than cowards masking themselves for thuggery. [30]

---

[29] TENNESSEE WHITE CAPS, *The Evening Sentinel*, July 16, 1891
[30] TREATS IT SERIOUSLY, *The Knoxville Journal*, August 26, 1891

Regardless of the actual inspiration for Whitecapping to manifest itself in Sevier County, it did, which resulted in the fabric of the country county getting ripped and twisted and torn into a place where people were held hostage by the night. Irrespective of when the manifestation began—a dark, new culture, faceless and without compassion got a foothold. It rolled with a mob's momentum and seemed to gain strength and vitality through collective evil. It traveled the dirt roads and canopied footpaths to wherever it had decided something needed fixing or a lesson needed to be taught—or a score needed to be settled, or a tenant kept in line. And it carried out its wicked justice in a most hideous fashion, as often as not on those least able to resist.

They called themselves White Caps.

It was a name that just a few years later would not be spoken so much as it would be spat into the Sevier County dust.

Exactly how the White Caps initially came to exist may have been lost to history. The most authoritative ones, those compiled during the actual events, do not really offer much of a clue; not surprising, since publishing that kind of detail in real time held a fairly significant potential for drawing the ire of the White Caps—then receiving threats of physical harm and actual physical harm—up to and including death itself.

Indeed, White Capping was a subject best left alone in Sevier County well into the second half of the 20th century, because first-generation descendants of those involved were still alive and still touchy about having their ancestor's legacies stained with lawlessness. That probably also accounts for the scarcity of any cohesive chronicle of the White Cap phenomenon.

Because there is no cohesive chronicle, establishing the season in which Whitecapping began in Sevier County is difficult, though it has generally been identified as "1892." There's at least one problem with that theory—according to Cas Walker, the comments made by an unnamed judge were:[31]

> "GENTLEMEN," SAID THE JUDGE as he pushed his plate back on the hotel dining room table, "Gentlemen, my court is hamstrung. You good citizens bring evidence against these *lewd women* into court each term. The grand jury returns indictments. But, when they come to trial, there's someone to swear them out."

If "good citizens" were bringing evidence against "lewd women into court each term," that seems to suggest it had been going on for a while. If it had been going on for a while, it seems likely the lewd women arrived sometime before the winter of 1891/1892 for a judge to use the phrase, "each term."

The Second Judicial Circuit contained the counties of Claiborne, Campbell, Grainger, Union, Hamblen, Jefferson, Cocke, Anderson and Sevier, and the Second Judicial Circuit Court judge was the Honorable W. R. Hicks. The earliest newspaper articles referencing Judge Hicks suggest he presided over cases in Sevier County from 1886 until March 1897, when Sevier County was placed under Knox County's Criminal Court jurisdiction under Judge T. A. R. Nelson, Jr. The Circuit Court terms in Sevier County began the third Monday in March, July and November. Terms generally ran until the docket was cleared.

One account of the White Cap formation is credited specifically to Judge Hicks, who was highly criticized publicly by Tom Davis for being too lenient on White Caps. Davis was quite outspoken in his belief that it was Judge Hicks whose loose comments from the bench was the genesis for the White Cap organization in Sevier county.[32]

---

[31] Walker, 1
[32] HAS TWO SIDES, *The Knoxville Tribune*, Knoxville, Tennessee, March 28, 1897

"Mr. Davis is of the opinion that Judge Hicks is not the proper man to deal with the Sevier County violators of the law and that the court should be held by a more determined man. He says that Judge Hicks has many friends among the white caps, and furthermore that the white caps were the outcome of a remark made by Judge Hicks from the bench *seven years ago*. The remark in question was in effect this: There were on trial some *lewd women* and the jury failed to convict any of them.. This Mr. Davis says made Judge Hick angry and he said in open court that if the juries would not convict these guilty people that the citizens should take the matter into their own hands."

There are a couple of items from this article worthy of consideration. Consider the time frame: "seven years ago" would have been 1890, quite a bit earlier than the prostitutes were believed to have moved to Emert's Cove/Copeland Creek. Davis was not appointed a deputy sheriff until 1894, so it makes one wonder how Davis would have been privy to such knowledge in 1890.

The Knoxville Tribune offered Judge Hicks two and a half columns in the March 29, 1897, edition to explain his perceived leniency when it came to holding White Caps accountable for their crimes.[33]

From Judge Hicks, himself:

"Over seven years ago, as I now remember, in a moment of anxiety over what I suppose was a refusal of a grand jury to make a presentment, or find an indictment, I said to them: 'Gentlemen, must this offense (speaking of a certain offense

---

[33] FROM JUDGE HICKS, *The Knoxville Tribune*, Knoxville, Tennessee, March 29, 1897

which, for reasons, I will not here name) go unpunished? If the courts of the country will refuse the citizen protection against such outrages, may we not expect the shot gun next? Will the husband long submit to such outrageous insults to the wife?"

Judge Hicks goes on to say he made this statement "in the impetuosity of a moment," which seems to indicate he acknowledged the recklessness of such a statement made from the bench. His words "refusal of a grand jury ..." may have planted a seed in a hearer or hearers of those words, who deemed it necessary to hijack the grand juries by using Justice of the Peace empaneled jurors.

Hicks used two and a half columns to make his case that he was a responsible jurist, and not a Whitecap supporter or sympathizer, either by action or inaction.

It has been suggested that about a dozen years prior to the Tipton and Wynn executions in July 1899, there was a deliberate effort on the part of Knoxville to shut down brothels.

"Most probably it started a dozen years earlier when, over in Knoxville, authorities began shutting down brothels, and, so the story goes, the women began relocating out into the country."[34]

If true, and the "lewd women" arrived around 1887, this would give a judge time to lament the fact that by 1890 he couldn't get convictions.

No transcript of the following statement has been found, but it is similar to Cas Walker's version, in that *a judge* made a suggestion in open court, supposedly following a charge to a just-seated grand jury.

"Gentlemen," a judge is alleged to have said, "we bring these women in from Copeland Creek (not too far from Emert's Cove) and charge them

---

[34] Ina Hughs, 'The Eyes of Midnight' recalls dark history in Sevier County, archive.knoxnews.com, June 25, 2016

with *lewdness*. But men who forsake their wives always come in and swear them out, lying to get an acquittal."

He then suggested some of them band together, disguise themselves with hoods and bed sheets and go to Copeland Creek. They should whip the women until they "straighten up and be the kind of women they should be. They are a disgrace to the community."

A third source traces the White Caps' formation to an offhand remark by *a judge* at a cafe luncheon in Sevierville, the county seat. The judge lamented that he could not get convictions against a half-dozen or so unnamed women who had apparently migrated from Knoxville and established a whorehouse in Emert's Cove.

But the judge is said to have told his luncheon companions the women always evaded charges or defeated conviction because witnesses—presumably the men who had patronized the business—would lie under oath, saying they had not been there. And because of the private nature of this commercial enterprise, their testimony was difficult-if-not-impossible to refute.

Furthermore, the men had additional motivation to absolve the women of culpability, so they would not have to return home and face their wives, should they testify for the prosecution.

One of the judge's lunch partners is alleged to have suggested that a band of men be formed to go to Copeland Creek and give the women a whipping and instructions to leave the county or face additional—and more stern—retribution.

There is no hard evidence any of these accounts were the genesis of White Capping in Sevier County—only hearsay.

Historically accurate? Unknown and presumably unknowable. In any case, any of these scenarios represent a judicial foul ball of immense proportions, if not downright conspiracy.

A seemingly overlooked cultural aspect of the entire episode is the misogynistic nature of the selective enforcement of community morals.

In other words, why were the women punished and not their clientele? Sadly, it reflects the male dominated society and societal institutions of the era. It is worth mentioning that women were not allowed to vote, sit on juries or hold office.

Regardless, the wayward women of Copeland Creek woke one morning, allegedly during the winter of 1891/1892, to find a bundle of hickory switches—also called withes—on their front steps. Attached was a note advising them to leave the community or face a whipping with the withes. It was signed by the "White Caps."

Another account says some of "the wives of the community, angry that their menfolk's attention had turned away from the hearth, formed a mob to protect their families and homes. Urged on by several men, the women went to the dwelling of each prostitute one night and laid bundles of hickory switches at the front doors with a note telling the occupants to leave the neighborhood or suffer a beating during a later visit. The messages were signed 'The White Caps.'"[35]

In either defiance or disbelief, the women remained.

But the White Caps were serious, and shortly made good on their threat, and the women got a thrashing. The White Caps left them with another warning that failure to flee would result in another, even more brutal beating. Having been made believers, the women retreated back from whence they came, where their potential customer base was greater, even if the competition for their services was, too.

And so it started, demonstrating that the road that leads to the moral high ground sometimes runs through the shadows in the valley of lawlessness.

Without a doubt the wayward women of Copeland Creek were on the south side of the law and imminently short of the glory by community standards. On the other hand, the White Cap response—irrespective of

---

[35]Cummings, p. 1

its moral righteousness—was assault, plain and simple. And entirely illegal.

And if it had stopped there, the story would be over. But it did not, and what started out as a fairly mild enforcement of Victorian values in an isolated, God-fearing community eventually degenerated into an unabated wave of crime with no moral underpinning whatsoever.

[36] Cover of Cas Walker's *The White Caps of Sevier County,* first published in 1937; The second edition was published 1974.

4

Sworn Allegiance

But as 1892 blossomed, the county was still a hardscrabble Appalachian enclave that depended much more on horses than it did on horsepower. The big news was the harlots that had settled into Copeland Creek and their harshly induced relocation. The White Caps, having achieved their goal and having avoided punishment, interpreted that as tacit approval of their actions by the community (community consensus). And, indeed, there were many in the community who no doubt harbored sympathy for the group, even if their methods were entirely unlawful.

Many Sevier Countians eventually joined the White Caps with no intention of beating anyone with a hickory withe, but did so for either economic or political gain.[37]

> "Soon merchants and mechanics joined the organization in order to attract business; and whitecaps began to take on the trappings of a mystic fraternal organization, like the Masons or

---

[37] Cummings, 19

Oddfellows, complete with secret meetings and signs, blood oaths, and ritual garb. Eventually, the justices and other local politicians identified themselves with the vigilantes at election time and sought their vote."

But it was a secret society, and those always attract an element that wants to belong somewhere, particularly if there were aspects of it that allowed the member the quiet knowledge that "I know something you don't." Whitecap numbers burgeoned to an estimated membership of between 650 and 1,500 members, partly because criminals joined the organization *after* they committed crimes, as a means of securing protection against arrest and prosecution.

The White Caps' organizational chart would have been a murky undertaking, had it ever been attempted. Unlike some later organized crime operations, this was a loose confederation wherein status and rank were likely never entirely clear even to members. Indeed, an organization that performs its function in the dark is especially hard to chart, even in the light of day.

In the absence of a true chain of command, specific titles—for individuals or bands of men—were fluid, except those who were called "raiders," and those who were called "supporters." The White Caps organization consisted of those two groups: "supporters," who were always there to provide bail money and legal fees for those who conducted the raids, the "raiders," and then to swear that the defendants were somewhere else, doing something else, with someone else.

Tradition says that only one man, the main man, had a specific title— actually two. He was the "Chief Mogul" or "High Cockalorum." A cockalorum is defined as "a self-important little man." If you were that guy in Sevier County you were respected by many and probably feared by all. But very few actually knew who you were, and that's the way you wanted it.

William Wynn, or Squire Wynn, could have been that person, as previously stated in our introduction. His family had the social status and connections, and his father, Elkanah M. Wynn had been High Sheriff of Sevier County. Squire Bill Wynn served as the superintendent of the county work farm, and as such would have had regular interactions with the county's criminal element. Through these regular interactions, it is conceivable that he leveraged his position to develop relationships, whereby the exchange of favors could have been the currency for criminal conduct.

In the same way that the White Caps' illegitimate entry into the court system through the Justices of the Peace went a long way toward removing legal liability for the organization's actions, another technical safeguard was added. The group might be White Caps, but they would not call themselves that.

They adopted the name Grave Yard Hosts, allowing plausible deniability if members were asked, "Are you a White Cap?"

The answer was, of course, "No." It was a distinction without a difference, for sure, but perhaps it made them feel better about themselves. They did not have to lie about their affiliation, even if they seemed to have no compunction at all about beating a woman half to death in the middle of the night for joining some man in bed, and tangling up the same kind of sheets the White Caps were cutting eyeholes in. A state law passed in 1897 in response to Sevier County's White Cap problem would remove the naming distinction, though the law was enacted after the Whitecapping reign of terror had self-destructed.

So White Cap membership had grown rapidly, particularly in the communities of Flat Creek, Catlettsburg, Pigeon Forge and the area around Sevierville. Prospective inductees were called on to swear a blood oath of secrecy and loyalty. One traditional account says that the following

26

oath[38] was administered with cocked White Cap pistols aimed at the new member, which suggests the entire oath and oath swearing ceremony were taken somewhat less than "freely and voluntarily":

The Oath

I do solemnly swear before God and man that if I reveal anything concerning our organization or anything we may do, the penalty shall be to receive one hundred lashes and leave the county within ten days or be put to death. Now I take this oath freely and voluntarily, and am willing to abide by the obligation in every respect. I further agree and swear before God that if I reveal anything concerning our organization, I will suffer my throat to be cut, my heart to shot out and my body to be burned; that I will forfeit my life, my property and all that I may have in this world and in the world to come: So help me God.

As membership grew, those who had taken such an oath included men of high stature and financial independence within the community, even officials of government, law enforcement and the legal profession.

So the beatings increased in number as the months went on, with no one prosecuted for what was assault at best, and attempted homicide at worst. They occurred almost nightly somewhere in Sevier County, most perpetrated against women—and sometimes men—accused of having relations with someone other than their lawfully wedded spouse.

The men responsible for these nighttime atrocities basked in the admiration of their neighbors in the light of day, and apparently little interest was invested in whether the allegations were true or rose to the level of being unlawful. An accusation of infidelity—to one's mate or to the community's standard of behavior—was enough to get you a

---

[38] Crozier, 9

nocturnal visit from faceless marauders, vigilantes who were prepared to impose their morality with an extension of The Authorized Version, that was about the length of a hickory withe.

Usually, the White Caps, having previously issued their wooden-bundle-wrapped written warning, would converge on a home in the middle of the night. They customarily battered in the door, dragged the offending individual out into the night, and two or more would hold his or her arms outstretched as their nightclothes were pulled up over their heads from behind. Then the lashes were delivered fiercely by one or more White Caps, most often beating the victim bloody and leaving him or her unconscious or nearly so, before vanishing into the darkness, their identities still unknown.

Arrests, when they did happen, almost never resulted in convictions. Plus, claims against the attackers were almost impossible to substantiate, because the victim would never see the faces of the attackers hidden inside their White Cap hoods—only their eyes. Even though the wearing of masks ostensibly provided the raiders plausible deniability, their identities were generally known through other affiliations in the community, such as the Odd Fellows lodges located in Sevierville and Pigeon Forge. The Sevierville Lodge met every Friday night and the Pigeon Forge Lodge met every Saturday night, and it is not a leap to believe that Whitecapping was on the agenda, whether officially or not. In a later chapter, you'll read about such an occurrence one Saturday night after a meeting at the Pigeon Forge Odd Fellows lodge.

The one Sevier County White Cap disguise known to survive is a fairly sophisticated example, with intricate needlework about the cylindrical head piece, mesh-covered eye holes and a frilly, out-of-character ruffle on the front. In all likelihood, however, most White Cap disguises were just sheets with holes cut for vision.

As the influence of the White Caps grew, politicians courted their favor, then reciprocated by failing to actively pursue their comrades to capture or properly prosecute them when they were hauled into court. White Caps were routinely selected for grand juries by the county court, making an indictment difficult to come by. And when it did occur, the White Caps would often be aware of it before the indictment was revealed in open court. The same thing applied to trials, where a White Cap in the jury box—and only men could serve on juries—secured at least a hung jury and a mistrial, if not an acquittal.

As a prospective juror was questioned, he might pass his right hand over his cheek, a signal that "I'm a White Cap." An attorney would then respond by passing his left hand over his cheek in like manner, signifying his comprehension and answering, "So am I." So the White Cap was duly selected and seated. Potential witnesses either perjured themselves in sympathy to the White Caps or were intimidated into doing so. Justice thus subverted, the rest of the court proceedings was all for show, and the White Caps' secrets remained secured.

The Russell Jenkins Incident[39]
April 25, 1892

As previously stated, Whitecapping in east Tennessee seemed to have begun in late 1891, but it seemingly permeated Sevier County far more than in any other east Tennessee county. One early documented White Cap incident involved a large group of vigilantes crossing over into Jefferson County to administer its particular and peculiar brand of morality enforcement. Russell Jenkins, an elderly man over seventy years of age and former preacher, was living with a widow woman who was not his wife.

---

[39] DISGRACEFUL, *The Knoxville Journal and Tribune*, Knoxville, Tennessee, April 26, 1892, Front Page

It is interesting to note that while he had been enjoying the aforementioned living arrangement for several years, the community at large had not intervened until the winter and spring of 1892.

Some weeks prior to the White Caps outrage perpetrated against Jenkins, he received a notice to leave the country, signed by the White Caps with "the usual skull and cross bones attachment."[40]

"The usual skull and crossbones attachment?"

DISGRACEFUL!

White Cap Outrage Perpe-
trated Near Dandridge.

A NUMBER OF MASKED MEN

Shoot Down an Old Man and
Then Badly Beat Him.

HIS BACK CUT INTO THREADS.

Again Warning Him to Leave
the Country They Sneak.

ONE OF THE WHITE CAPS WOUNDED

Residents of the Vicinity Indignant at the Outrage.

The notice did not achieve its desired result, and Jenkins armed himself and promised to give the masked cowards a warm welcome should they pay him a nocturnal visit. When the crowd of White Caps awakened him he fired two volleys into their midst, grievously injuring at least one of the intruders. The marauders returned fire, and Jenkins was

---

[40] *The Knoxville Journal and Tribune*, August 3, 1892, page 3

struck in the head and face. Once incapacitated, Jenkins was surrounded, dragged into his yard, and subjected to "a most unmerciful beating, his back being literally cut into threads."

It was further reported that "some hours later a group of twenty-three men, all heavily masked and armed, crossed the river at Douglass' Ferry, one of the men bleeding profusely."

Another incident previously cited in this book took place during the overnight hours of Saturday, May 14 and Sunday, May 15, 1892. It seems a group of White Caps had previously warned an unnamed man, and he was ready for them when they arrived to administer their cowardly violence.

WHITE CAPS AGAIN.

SEVIER COUNTY OUTLAWS MEET A WARM RECEPTION.

One of Their Number Killed and Another Wounded.

The White Caps in Sevier county continue their depredations but they met with a warm reception Saturday night.

They visited the home of a man who had been "warned," and he was prepared for them. He was hidden in the brush near his house, and when they opened the door he shot at them, using a shotgun loaded with buckshot, killing one man and wounding another. The White Caps retreated, taking their dead and wounded with them.

Cal Jones has since been under the care of a physician, who has been treating him for a gunshot wound, and while he will not admit it, it is believed he was one of the night riders of Saturday night. The man who was killed was James Free, and he was buried that night by his comrades.

The white cap movement originated in Emmert's cove two or three months ago, and was headed by two men and a number of married women who sought to take revenge upon men who had proved false to their marriage vows. The cove had been overrun with women of ill-repute, and caused men who had before led upright lives to go astray. The settlement was soon cleared of the obnoxious inhabitants but the mania spread to other parts of the county, and men and women have been whipped by the score, but the killing of Saturday night was the first since night riding began.

Continued on next page

An organization called the "Blue Bills" was formed sometime ago to resist the White Caps, but its members so far have shown the "white feather," for they have never dared to meet their enemies.

Rosie Jenkins was the last victim before the attempted raid of Saturday night. She was charged with being the mistress of a man in official position and she was warned to leave the county, but refused to obey She was taken from her house one night last week and beaten nearly to death. Her paramour has also been threatened, but he does not seem to be in any way intimidated.

Everybody is afraid to do anything toward having the outlaws brought to justice, for fear of suffering at their hands but it is whispered that the leader of the gang is a Justice of the peace. Over five hundred revolvers have been sold throughout the county within the last two months, the purchasers being citizens of the highest standing, who fear that they may unwittingly incur the displeasure of white caps, and be visited by them and if such happens to be the case, they want to be prepared for the occasion.

A wholesale killing is looked for at any time for the people are becoming aroused, the officers have thus far done nothing to stop the outrages, and the people are determined to see what they can do.

Several things stand out about the previously cited article above, dated 18 May 1892. These articles illustrate how the details often changed from day to day, and even newspaper to newspaper.

WHITE CAPS IN SEVIER.

An Intended Victim Fires Into a Lawless Band.

One Man Killed and Another Fatally Wounded—The County Excited and More Bloodshed Probable.

KNOXVILLE, May 17.—[Special.]—Information reaches this city to-night of a bloody White Cap affair in Sevier County Sunday morning before day. A band of White Caps went to the home of a man to whip him. He showed fight, and fired on the crowd with a Winchester. John Fell was instantly killed and Jim Jones seriously and probably fatally wounded. The entire county is in a state of turmoil, and more bloodshed is certain to follow. The anti-White Cap feeling is spreading, but the White Caps declare they will have vengeance at all costs.

The article below, dated 19 May 1892, demonstrates how quickly some prominent Sevier Countians responded to squelch news about Whitecapping. Could their response suggest an attempted cover-up of Whitecapping activities?

> **No Foundation for It.**
> A delegation of Sevier county citizens composed of Wm. Trotter, postmaster at Trotters postoffice, Fred Emmert, a merchant at Sevierville, M. C. and L. S. Trotter, called at THE JOURNAL office yesterday and requested to enter an absolute, and unqualified denial of the sensational report in yesterday morning's Tribune of the sensational work of White Caps in Sevier county and the murder of Free. There is no foundation for such a story and the gentlemen wish the story denied in justice to Sevier county people.

The Murder of Eli Williamson
July 14, 1892

> Two murders in Sevier County last week. Wm. Sneed killed Eli Williamson for saying he had swore a lie. And Thos. Reed killed Robert Louis. The cause was some trouble over a cow.

July nights are sticky in Emert's Cove, and on one of those evenings early on in the White Cap saga, a group of the anonymous withe-bearers gathered outside the home of Julia Ramsey, intent on meting out to her a portion of their extralegal punishment for transgressions unknown. What the White Caps did not know, however, was that the woman was not alone. What Eli Williamson and Henry Proffitt were doing at her house, no one can say. But they were there, and they were armed.

As was their custom, the White Caps violently breached the cabin door, but that was only the first line of defense. Williamson and Proffitt made up the second line. Unexpectedly, the White Caps were met with gunfire and retreated from what was supposed to be a simple thrashing of a defenseless woman. In the gun battle, one of Williamson's bullets found the leg of Lewallen Sneed, one of the attackers. Mountainfolk being mountainfolk, a clannish bunch by nature, something of a feud quickly developed. The Sneeds were incensed at one of their own being wounded, without regard to the fact he had conspired to commit assault, and was on a mission to do so.

A few days after the skirmish, Lewallen Sneed's brother, William, and Houston Romines were seen walking down the road near Williamson's dilapidated log home at the foot of Webb's Mountain on Emert's Cove Road, 14 miles from Sevierville. William Sneed had a rifle.

A narrative of the events has Sneed going to the front door while Romines, wielding a long-blade knife, slinked around back.

This time, Williamson was unarmed. Realizing his predicament, Williamson ran to the rear of the house and tried to surrender. Without remorse, Sneed took aim and exacted his revenge. Williamson died a few hours later, the victim in the first killing directly attributable to the White Caps.

The residents of Emert's Cove had very quickly had enough and banded together in opposition to the White Caps under the leadership of John Sam Springs, the postmaster for Emert's Cove, who stated for the record:

"Any man or set of men who would go *at the dead hours of midnight* under the cover of darkness, with masks on their faces, and drag a poor defenseless woman from her home and lash her back is a base coward and not worthy of citizenship."

Such a man should be justifiably deprived of his freedom under the law. But that is apparently not what happened in this case.

William Sneed, it is said, fled across the mountains into North Carolina, and there was no indication that by the turn of the century he had faced a courtroom in connection with the killing of Eli Williamson.

34

5

Colonel John Sam Springs

Colonel John Sam Springs has not gotten the credit he earned, and deserves, for his part in the eradication of Whitecapping in Emert's Cove. According to E. W. Crozier, "John S. Springs, who led the opposition in Emert's Cove, was a man of great courage, backed up with an iron will and invincible determination."[41]

In a very real sense Springs' participation in this saga bookends the reign of terror in Sevier County. He first stood in defiance of them in Emert's Cove in 1892, then seven years later placed the hoods over the heads of Catlett Tipton and Pleas Wynn on 5 July 1899, then tightened the nooses around their necks. In the interim, Springs served as the Jury Foreman on the March 1897 grand jury that returned a "true bill" against James Catlett Tipton and Pleasant D. Wynn for murder, and against W. R. "Bob" Catlett and Bob Wade for accessory. Legend also has it that the nooses cut from around Catlett Tipton's and Pleas Wynn's necks ended up in Springs' possession.

---

[41] Crozier, 85

No one seems to know from whence John Springs received the title "Colonel." Mae Stamey Owenby, a Former Tennessee State Representative and Great-granddaughter of Springs, speculates the title may have been honorific in nature. That, and the fact he insisted upon his death that he not be buried in a Christian cemetery because of his role as Hangman in the Catlett Tipton and Pleas Wynn executions, make Colonel John S. Springs perhaps the most enigmatic character in the White Caps saga.

John Sam Springs was born in Buncombe County, North Carolina on 18 October 1856, and married Mary Sitton in the same county around 1876. They had one child, Bertha Mae Springs. John and Mary separated and divorced, and Mary took Bertha Mae to Greeneville, South Carolina, where they lived with an older couple and Mary worked in a dress shop. Unknown to Mary, John sent the couple $25 and asked them to place Bertha Mae on a train to Asheville. Bertha Mae remembered having a sign around her neck, which she could not read, and arrived in Asheville. She never saw her mother again.

The John Sam Springs Family, circa 1890.
John Sam Springs, Bertha Mae Springs, John Springs' second wife.
Photo courtesy of Mae Stamey Owenby.

John Sam Springs settled in Emert's Cove around 1890, and was appointed Postmaster of Emert's Cove in 1891. If you follow the timeline of Whitecapping in Sevier County as reported in newspaper articles, members of the organization first called themselves "The White Caps of Emert's Cove". Recall that the first mention of "Blue Bills" was in the May 18, 1892 article, and the last documented Whitecapping incident in Emert's Cove appears to have been the murder of Eli Williamson in July 1892.

Because of how the White Caps saga unfolded, it is highly plausible that the Blue Bills' founder was John Sam Springs, and that his homestead was their original headquarters.

Historic John Springs Homestead

Home was built around 1890. Home was Headquarters for the Blue Bills, an early law enforcement group. John was a prominent citizen of Emert's Cove and best known for performing the last public hanging in Sevier County around 1900. Land was also home to native Americans and was their hunting grounds before Euro American Settlers.

John Springs was a man of courage and conviction. He helped stop a reign of killing and terror by the "White Caps" in the late 1800s. An unsung Sevier County hero.

Legend has it there were a number of pitched battles between the White Caps and Blue Bills at the Springs' homestead, as evidenced by the bullet holes, gun port and peep hole in the doors of the home.

37

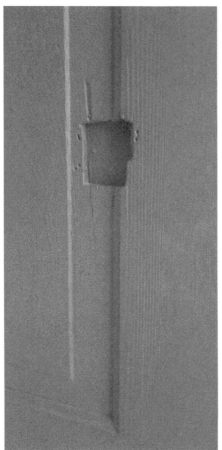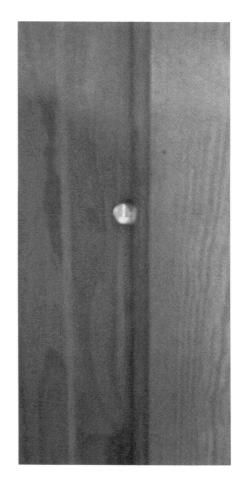

Photos inside the John Springs' home,
taken during the tour conducted by Colonel Vince Ingle.

Evidently the burden of having served as the Hangman in Sevier County's last legal, public hanging on 5 July 1899, was too great for Colonel Springs. Even though the Emert Cemetery in Emert's Cove is a short walk from the Springs' homestead, he felt unworthy of being buried in a Christian cemetery, and was buried in an unmarked grave on his property. The grave was eventually marked, but the grave marker that marked the exact location of John Sam Springs' final resting place has been lost to time.

Colonel John Sam Springs Memorial Cemetery

Final resting place of Colonel John Sam Springs. He performed the last public hanging in Sevier County on July 5, 1898, at the courthouse. After the hangings, he felt unworthy to be buried in Emert's Cove Cemetery. He was a gentle man who showed kindness to children.

Colonel Springs must not have wanted a haircut. When I first asked Mae Stamey Owenby what she could tell me about this picture, she said, "I can tell you everything about it, and my nephew Mark has the original." Mark Stamey was generous enough to mail it to Mae, so that I could scan it. I inserted the picture "as-is," as a testament to its authenticity. John Sam Springs, seated; Barber's name is Cantrell; and John's third wife Martha Whaley is holding the pistol in jest.

Mae Stamey Owenby and her brother, Leonard Stamey, displaying the same pistol Martha Whaley Springs held in the original picture.

Colonel Robert Vinsant Ingle, DDS, pointing out the same window underneath which John Sam Springs sat while getting his haircut.

There were some dots of the White Cap saga in Sevier County we never were able to connect until we discovered the Cummings thesis.

John Sam Springs evidently took a stand against Whitecapping in Emert's Cove, yet Whitecapping spread quite efficiently and rather rapidly in the other Civil Districts in Sevier County.

If you recall, Cummings doesn't mince words in his thesis, and is particularly candid in his description of how, and how quickly, the White Cap movement mutated from an organization ostensibly begun to uphold and enforce community standards, and metastasized into marauding bands of criminals.

> Shortly, after the charivari of the prostitutes in Emert's Cove, whitecap gangs were organized by justices of the peace who were able to protect their men by dismissing the whitecap cases in their court for lack of evidence. On the few cases that were bound over to the circuit court, the justices were still able to intercede for the night riders by selecting fellow whitecaps to serve on grand and petit juries.[42]

If "White Cap gangs were organized by justices of the peace ...," then what we have in Sevier County is at best corruption and collusion, and at the worst organized crime.

To better understand the connection between the justices of the peace and prominent, wealthy landowners, Cummings goes on to say:

> Within a short time, whitecap gangs were being sponsored by wealthy farmers who helped the vigilantes by guaranteeing their bail and providing counsel during court proceedings.[43]

---

[42] Cummings, 19
[43] Ibid

While E. W. Crozier, Cas Walker and William Joseph Cummings III all refer to the extralegal activities of the White Caps beyond enforcing community behavioral standards as "ku-kluxing," there is no evidence any of the Whitecapping in Sevier County was racially motivated. Cummings explains better than any other source what the true nature of Whitecapping in Sevier County ultimately became:[44]

> As a result of the "new ku-kluxing," crimes, feuds, and vendettas, raged on unchecked in Sevier County in the name of a non-existent consensus that circumvented justice and destroyed the "fragile social equilibrium" that insured honor within the community.

The depth, breadth, height and width of the corruption is unimaginable, so it is necessary to take a deeper look at the Justice of the Peace legal system in Sevier County and Whitecapping, that organization that originally rose up to enforce community behavioral standards, which ultimately became a Brood of Vipers and Den of Thieves.

---

[44] Cummings, 21

6

"Justice for the Plaintiff"[45]

To fully comprehend how the White Caps managed to infiltrate, permeate, and therefore compromise the legal system in Sevier County, it is essential for the reader to know the degree to which the Justice of the Peace system in Sevier County had been bastardized, or illegitimized.

Justices of the Peace, or Squires, were officials elected in each of Sevier County's Civil Districts for six year terms, and that in and of itself is not a bad thing. But in Sevier County, and one might conclude that the practice was performed similarly in other counties, Justices of the Peace were typically members of, or were aligned with, the most prominent families in a Civil District, or with other politically connected constituents within those Civil Districts. The existing source material about Whitecapping in Sevier County is replete with Justices of the Peace who came from some of the more prominent families from that era, which not coincidentally are some of the more prominent families in the modern era.

The role of the Justice of the Peace, within each Civil District, was to adjudicate cases more along the lines of misdemeanors, those crimes in which little property damage or minor personal injury were involved. By

---

[45] Cummings, 6

hearing and ruling on these cases, Justices of the Peace were ostensibly able to keep the County Court docket clear for cases involving significant property damage, or cases of homicide and other serious personal injury.

Here's where the nature of the Justice of the Peace system and the County Court becomes more nefarious, and for a few reasons.

First, Justices of the Peace typically had no proper legal training, and it was not a salaried position, so it was quite common for the person who brought the case to the Justice of the Peace to pay the Justice of the Peace. Justices were required to prepare and turn in annual reports of proceedings, but there were no standardized forms, and there were no requirements as to how much or how little they were required to report. This is why the legal community mockingly referred to the Justice of the Peace system as "Justice for the Plaintiff".

The County Court was made up of, if you can believe this, Justices of the Peace from the Civil Districts. Each Civil District had two Justices of the Peace represented on the County Court, other than the Civil District in which the county seat was located. This Civil District had three Justices of the Peace on the County Court.

Therefore, the Justices of the Peace not only performed gatekeeping duties in terms of the cases that made it to the Grand Juries, they also made up the County Court. The significance of making up the County Court is evidenced by the fact that the County Court empaneled the Grand Juries, thereby assuring White Caps were well-represented when the cases were heard. This explains why "true bills," or indictments, were rarely returned when cases were heard against White Cap defendants.

The circuit court typically heard more serious cases, those that involved grand thefts and grievous bodily harm or murder. If the grand jury returned an indictment, or a true bill was brought against a defendant, it was then heard by the circuit court judge. At trial, the case was heard by the petit jury, consisting of twelve men, who considered the evidence and returned any number of verdicts. Until the passage of the so-called Anti-

Whitecap Law in 1897, petit juries were easily infiltrated by White Caps. And the presiding judge could always adjudicate cases in ways that meant juries never heard the evidence.

Understanding the Sevier County legal system of the 1890s is paramount to understanding the lawlessness that ruled that era, and how the corruption of the Justices of the Peace was the breeding ground for vipers and thieves.

The narrative of the White Caps saga we first encountered goes something like this: a group of prostitutes moved into the vicinity of Emert's Cove/Copeland Creek in 1892, a judge lamented the fact he could not get convictions against them for lewdness, and an offhand remark by said judge resulted in unknown persons masking themselves, leaving a note with a bundle of hickory withes warning the prostitutes to leave or suffer a beating with the withes. The prostitutes essentially called their bluff, the withes were administered and the prostitutes left. Then, because this method seemed to have been effective in upholding community standards of behavior, the White Caps organized themselves and spread throughout Sevier County for the same reason: upholding Victorian morals and community standards of behavior and conduct.

It seems more likely the prostitutes arrived sometime in at least 1891, which gave the aforementioned series of events long enough to transpire prior to the January 1892 newspaper article that first mentioned the "White Caps of Emert's Cove".[46]

Because Whitecapping was illegal in its genesis, the only natural evolution for such an organization was to continue a spiral into progressively more and more lawlessness.

We believe the time lapse between John Sam Springs and the Blue Bills eradicating the White Caps from Emert's Cove and the county-wide spread of Whitecapping took much less time than previously suggested.

---

[46] WHITE CAPS IN SEVIER, January 27, 1892

And we also believe the motive for the spread of Whitecapping changed as well, from the enforcement of community standards of conduct and behavior to something even more systemic and sinister. When the criminal element in Sevier County flocked to their ranks, they eventually became nothing more than a Brood of Vipers and Den of Thieves.

7

The Breedens: A Turning Point
May 1893

While John Sam Springs and the good folks of Emert's Cove had apparently been effective in eradicating the White Caps, word had evidently spread and found the ears of those who thought Whitecapping means and methods were justifiable ways to deal with perceived breaches of community consensus. Still in its early stages, when dealing with perceived immoral activity between consenting partners, the righteous indignation of the White Caps turned the sins of adultery and fornication into crimes that left people physically maimed or worse. To wit:

Sevier County nights in May can still bring a chill, even if the mountain summer is only a few weeks away. At age 53, Mary Elizabeth Breeden was a widowed mother struggling to provide for herself and four of her children. The eldest, Jesse, 24, was the male presence there, and he had three sisters, Mary (also known as Belle), 20, Martha, 18, and Nancy 11. The word around Jones Cove was that the two older Breeden girls, both easy on the eyes, were spreading their sweetness a little too indiscriminately around the countryside. Mary Breeden, however, was not included in the rumors of sexual indiscretion.

Darkness brought a silence to the cove, broken only by the bullfrogs and the katydids and footsteps outside the windows. The Breedens were awakened.

"Oh! Jess, Oh! Jess, get up, we want to see you," came the cry from the captain of the band.

Jesse had assumed the mantle of household protector in the absence of a father, and perhaps had not remembered in his drowsiness that he had left his pistol at Jesse Robinson's gunsmith shop for repair.

He imprudently opened the door without challenging the identity of the caller outside, and was confronted by a yard full of armed White Caps, who had the drop on him when he opened the door. He was decisively outmatched.

Eight men entered the small house, and without much fanfare dragged a screaming Belle Breeden out into the chill in her nightclothes.

There had been no advance warning of this invasion, no bundle of withes with a note attached. But that technicality did not prevent the faceless attackers from carrying out the task at hand.

Four of the men took control of Jesse, covering him with their guns.

The other four advanced on Belle, stretching her arms in opposite directions in a crucifixion-style posture, rendering her completely defenseless. The other two pulled her nightgown over her head from the back and began laying on the lashes, this time with knotty black gum withes. Each swing of the branches produced a whistling sound followed by a sickening, fleshy thwack and a painful scream from Belle.

Blow followed blow, dozens of them, and each more violent than the last.

The ends of the withes, thin as wool yarn but much more destructive to the skin, lashed and slashed her back, turning it into an agonizing, bloody mosaic. The more she tried to escape, the more severe the beating became.

Mary Breeden pleaded with the men, in the name of God, for mercy for her daughter, but the White Caps only invoke the name of the same deity to rebuke her.

"Goddamn you. Hush! It will be your time next."[47]

And then for Belle it was over, except for the hideous pain and a gown stained with blood. She was led, on the edge of unconsciousness, back into the house.

Next on the White Caps' victim list was Martha, who was whipped in like fashion, but only a little less severely. This beating was as rhythmic as the first, punctuated by the girl's wailing and her mother's calls for mercy.

But mercy was not part of the plan—neither for the girls, nor for their mother.

Mary Breeden was brought to the whipping ground with tears for her daughters streaming down her face. Now she had to beg mercy for herself.

Beseeching her tormentors for mercy having proved ineffective, she now hurled invectives at them, calling them cowards for their deeds and protesting that her daughters had not done what they were accused of. Maybe that is why her beating was even more savage than the previous two.

As his mother endured her whipping Jesse wept. He was helpless to stop it, though once he attempted to break free of his captors and intervene. But that only caused the bandits to tighten their grip, to the point where one gun barrel nearly touched his face.

In that moment, Jesse heard and recognized the distinctive sound of his own revolver being cocked by one of the attackers. Maybe Jesse Robinson was one of these White Caps?

The licks and lashes kept coming until Mary was barely able to cry out any more. At this point, one of the masked nightriders emerged from

---

[47] Crozier, 181

among his comrades and called a halt to the proceedings. He had had enough.

He stepped to the front.

"Don't strike her another lick," he commanded. "I know 'is old lady … and she don't deserve treatment like 'is here."

An argument ensued among the criminals on whether to heed the warning or not, and as they were about to resume their tortuous task, Mary Breeden's defender again asserted himself.

"I'll shoot the head off'n the first man who strikes her another lick, if'n I die the next minute."

Maybe it was the bravery or the authoritative leadership. Maybe the strength of the voice or simply the threat that any further loss of Mary Breeden's blood would result in White Cap blood being blended with hers on the ground. In any case, Mary's whipping was over. She was barely conscious and bleeding badly from dozens of open wounds on her back as she was led back into the house.

Her nightgown was soaked in blood, and her long hair had fallen down over her shoulders and become matted in the gore.

The Breeden's horrifying night ended with the clop of horse hooves galloping away into the night.

Next morning as word of the incident spread, anger and sympathy rolled across Jones Cove like a summer storm.

Neighbor women arrived to help, as they always did when a family was in crisis. They soaked cloths in warm water to release Mary's hair from the dried blood on her back. They bound her wounds and those of Belle and Martha.

The menfolk got details of the attack from Jesse, whose mental anguish was nearly as tangible—and visible—as the welts and gashes on the backs of his sisters and mother. On the ground outside the home were bloody withes with strands of hair still attached.

Jones Cove collectively arose in outrage. Cursing of the White Caps, prior to this kept to one's self, now echoed freely through the hills.

Mary Breeden was so badly beaten that she never again left her bedroom. She lingered in misery for three months.

Around the first of August, a young physician of some skill and a man gaining influence throughout Sevier County, rode 14 miles to Mary Breeden's home for a house call. Her wounds having been inflicted with unclean black gum branches, her weakened body had to fight infection on its own, without the aid of medicines.

After an examination, the doctor told her there was nothing he could do to save her and that her time was short. Mary identified the "Ferguson boys" as being responsible for wounds which resulted in her death, which she succumbed to on August 4, 1893. Hers was the only whipping that was known to be fatal.

A counterinsurgency had formed early on in the White Caps saga, an organization formed to fight the White Caps on their own ground, with methods they could understand and a determination just as resolute. A man of means who had been moved by a close-up view of Mary Breeden's death became the leader and financier of the Blue Bills as a result.

His title was not as goofy as "Cockalorum." It was a lot more respectable. It was doctor.

Dr. James A. Henderson.

8

A Rising Opposition

As the summer of the heinous Breeden incident faded into autumn and winter, a small but scattered outlaw army was still imposing injustices on Sevier County's citizens who were perceived to be behaving immorally. But also fading was the White Caps' role as the moral conscience and disciplinary action council of the county.

For one thing, a line had been crossed.

It was one thing to kill Eli Williamson. In a mountain-justice sort of way, that could be rationalized based both on the male victim's ability to take care of himself, and the fact that in the end it was a not-uncommon family feud that actually took his life.

But Mary Breeden was a woman. Her family was not feuding with anybody, and these anonymous, cowardly bastards had beaten her to death in a horribly brutal fashion. That changed the equation in the minds of some, who quickly withdrew their encouragement where the White Caps were concerned.

What had started out as an extralegal means to make some women of ill-repute skedaddle back to Knoxville, and to bring some wayward women back into alignment with the King James Version, had suddenly taken on a life without moral justification.

There were no allegations that Mary Breeden was having relations with a man she wasn't married to. She was just the mother of two pretty girls who may have been, and there were serious questions as to whether Martha was any more guilty than her mother.

Law enforcement at the time was at best ineffective in combating the White Caps, and most likely was part of the problem. Sheriff George DeLozier, who served from 1890-94, may have been a reluctant enforcer, which amounted to passive support of Whitecapping. It is not much of a leap, then, to imagine that some of his deputies were likely affiliated.

In a rural county like Sevier, that selective enforcement would amount to a monumental dereliction of duty. But then no one was prepared to call the sheriff or anyone else to account, for fear of becoming the White Caps' next victim. And for that matter, to whom could the informant turn for help?

The Breeden nightmare left a bitter taste in the mouths of many who now decided that maybe this White Cap locomotive had gone off the rails. How far that sentiment extended beyond Jones Cove is hard to say, but it did include the physician who felt powerless to stop Mary Breeden's slow and painful death.

Dr. Henderson was only in his early 30s, but he had gained considerable respect in Sevier County through his medical practice, and as a leading thinker and doer in the community. Mary Breeden's death had been a personal affront.

The doctor was born just a couple of months after the Civil War began, and was just short of his 20th birthday when he married the former Mary Emma Montgomery, who died young.

Henderson lived on East Main Street in Sevierville, near the current site of the Atchley Funeral Home.

Physicians are, by nature, uncomfortable with suffering, which is one reason they embark on that career. So Mary Breeden's killing was a source of outrage, because it did not have to happen. And though the specific individuals who caused her death might not be identifiable, the umbrella organization they belonged to was. And Dr. Henderson made it his quest to thwart the White Caps at every turn, if possible.

Somewhere at its core, there is logic in the concept that a vigilante problem can be addressed by a vigilante solution. That if the law could not or would not rip the sheet off the White Cap, expose his identity and compel him to face the consequences of his hateful actions, then a robust opposition must do it for them.

After all, that is what gave birth to the White Cap organization in the first place. Dr. Henderson knew that. Thus the good doctor soon became the driving force behind the Blue Bills, who had one job and one only— get in the way of the White Caps and impede their actions any way possible—even if that required armed opposition.

Make no mistake, if the White Caps were outside the circle of the law, the Blue Bills were just as guilty. No, they did not target ordinary folk for minor indiscretions, and their posture was one of defense rather than attack. But in some cases Blue Bill tactics rolled dangerously close to— and, indeed, beyond—the line that runs between protecting the weak and assault, conspiracy or both.

There was blood. There was loss of life. Violence begat violence.

For some period of time almost no one in Sevier County knew whom to trust. The unaligned citizens were afraid of being victimized by the White Caps, who were afraid of being targeted by the Blue Bills, who must have had some trepidation about a law enforcement apparatus that had an incestuous relationship with the enemy.

It was a carousel of caution and distrust, with everybody glancing over his or her shoulder, looking to see who's looking.

The Blue Bills never numbered more than a couple hundred, it is thought, but then it's not like there was a roster to check, either. And on a defensive mission into the countryside, they never attempted to hide their identity. Nor did they have a code of secrecy or some oath to die for the cause.

What they did have was intelligence, both the kind attributed to their Cockalorum-equivalent, and the kind derived by having double agents in the camp of the adversary.

The Blue Bills likely got their information about planned White Cap escapades the old fashioned way—they bought it—the money presumably coming from the affluent, young physician. Cockalorums and oaths about having one's heart shot out generated only so much loyalty, and a few bucks had a way of dissolving much of that loyalty.

There is little to indicate where the name "Blue Bill" came from. Some say it was based on a hat they wore, but there is not much to validate that claim. Maybe it was just a name to distinguish them from White Caps. And one of the features of a cap is a bill. But there's no validation for that, either.

Headgear notwithstanding, the Blue Bills, usually outnumbered, seemed to have better information, better firepower and a stronger will to halt the White Caps than the White Caps had to overcome the resistance and continue with their nightly raids and beatings.

The two groups circled each other like angry felines for a time, with armed engagement seeming inevitable.

The Murder of Bruce Llewellyn, or Was It a Suicide?
April 1894

The murder of Bruce Llewellyn was reported in the Crozier book as an episode in the Whitecap saga, but even in that account the writer says, "At the funeral it was whispered around that he had been killed by one of the White-caps, but everybody seemed to be afraid to talk on the subject."[48]

One lingering question about the Llewellyn murder has always been, what was the source for reporting that Llewellyn was ambushed by *two* White Caps?

As you'll see, it was reported in the newspapers that Llewellyn committed suicide, so the truth may never be proven definitively.

Bruce Llewellyn was a White Cap, 24 years and five days old and full of youthful defiance and bravado. Some of his comrades had given notice that they intended to turn their vengeance on Llewellyn's mother. Membership apparently had no privileges.

Hannah Llewellyn was the mother of seven and had never been married, which would have been common knowledge in the area for at least a couple of decades. But now it became inexplicably important to punish her for her long-ago immoral behavior.

Bruce Llewellyn, however, declared that he would see to it that his Mama would suffer no retribution from the White Caps, even though he was among their number.

Multiple White Cap forays to carry out their mission were thwarted by residents and officers, who were obviously being tipped off in advance. That could not be tolerated. The White Caps' focus narrowed to Bruce Llewellyn, because he alone had reason to stop the attack.

It had to be him. He had betrayed his oath.

Some type of meeting was called for April 29, 1894, to draw Llewellyn away from home. The route to the meeting took him down Flat Creek Road, three miles east of Sevierville, past Millican Grove Church on the north side of the road, across from a thick forest of oak and pine. The night was starless, and Llewellyn took a path through the dark woods southward toward his destination.

---

[48] Crozier, 82

But along that path, two White Caps were hidden in the undergrowth, probably undisguised because they knew their victim was not going to be able to identify them.

A rustling sound in the brush was followed by a shotgun blast that hit Llewellyn in the head and dropped him instantly. His body was found the next day by two small boys who were on their way to a mill.

SEVIER'S NEW TRAGEDY.

BRUCE LLEWELLYN ACCIDENTALLY KILLED HIMSELF YESTERDAY.

John Mullandore Was Slightly Better Last Night.

Sevier county came to the front yesterday with another tragic death, which followed closely on the heels of Friday's shooting affray.

About four miles north of Sevierville, near the place known as Milligan's church yard, parties going along the public road discovered the body of a man lying prostrate in the road, at an early hour yesterday morning.

The man proved to be Bruce Llewellyn, a popular young farmer who resides but a short distance from where his body was found.

It was at first believed that the man had been murdered. Underneath his body was found a double-barreled shotgun, one barrel of which had been discharged.

A coroner's inquest was held and evidence brought out by it went to show conclusively that Llewellyn had met his death accidentally. He had carried his gun by a strap thrown over his shoulder and it is very probable that while in this position one barrel was accidentally discharged, the contents of which tore the back part of his head off, causing instant death. A verdict in accordance with these facts was rendered.

RIVERS OF BLOOD

Flow in the Good Old County of Sevier.

Bruce Llewellyn Found Dead in the Road Today.

A Supposition That he Was Murdered. John Mullandore and His Father shot by Capt. R. A. Montgomery—The Young Man May Recover.

From Saturday's Daily.

Early this morning several farmers passing along the road four miles north of Sevierville, in Sevier county, came across the body of a man lying in the middle of the road. Their first supposition was that he was a drunken sleeper, but closer investigation showed that the man was dead.

Underneath the prostrate man was a shotgun, one barrel of which had been fired. An ugly gun shot wound in his breast was the evident cause of his death.

The man was Bruce Llewellyn, a young farmer, 20 years of age, whose home is near the place where his body was found.

The report of the tragedy received at Sevierville today indicates that it is a foul murder, and that the gun was placed under the man's body in order to divert suspicion from the murderers. It was reported that Llewellyn had no gun when he left home, but that he did have some money and a watch. When his clothing were searched, the valuables were missing. There is an air of mystery about the terrible affair, which has produced great excitement all through Sevier county, where Llewellyn is well known.

If it can be substantiated that no murder was committed, it will still be a question whether the death was accidental or with suicidal intent.

> A coroner's jury in Sevier county held an inquest over Bruce Llewellyn, whose tragic death was reported in Saturday's Sentinel, and decided that he accidentally shot himself.

Newspaper articles from April 1894 report the death of Bruce Llewellyn, but a coroner's jury ultimately decided Llewellyn accidentally shot himself.

As Llewellyn was buried in Alder Branch Cemetery two days after the killing, people in the area suspected White Cap involvement, but they were disinclined to say it too loudly.

Later information indicated that Llewellyn was not the one who was thwarting the attack on his mother, but another in the group who may have been passing along information to the newly formed Blue Bills. That did not help Llewellyn, though. Vigilante injustices are often irrevocable in nature.

The Llewellyn killing represented a new level of retribution, a targeted murder. This was not just giving a lashing to a group of harlots, women whose social status was already pretty low. On those missions, you don't have to squint much to see the White Caps actually celebrating their action with whoops and laughter and more than a few slugs of barleycorn.

No, Llewellyn was a man. He could vote and serve on juries and hold office, and his punishment was final.

Trouble is that there was no one to speak up on Llewellyn's behalf. Half the population feared the White Caps as if they were an occupying army, and hundreds of others remained silent after having sworn acceptance of a graphically revolting death if they didn't. If raising a protest against the organization could get your brains splattered in the dark forest, it was probably smarter to keep one's mouth shut.

9

The Blue Bills Assert Themselves

In a previously cited newspaper article, it was reported that up to that point the Blue Bills had "so far shown the 'white feather'" to the White Caps, "for they have never dared to meet their enemies."[49] Dr. Henderson's leadership and financial support evidently emboldened the Blue Bills, and they gradually and more effectively engaged the White Caps.

Laura Rose opened the door of her Nunn's Cove home one morning, and a bundle of hate and fear fell inside, attached to a crudely handwritten note that addressed her by name. "Laura Rose, you better get out of this house in five days or we'll give you 75 licks."

It was signed by the Sevier County White Caps.

The woman lived there with her children, ages 4 and 6, and the nature of her supposed transgression was not preserved for later generations, nor are there easily discovered records of her living in Sevier County. Her story is one delivered by word of mouth—not hers, and not until a few

---

[49] WHITE CAPS AGAIN, *The Knoxville Tribune*, May 18, 1892

decades after the events. But there is a vein of truthfulness that bears exploration.

Laura Rose's discovery that morning sent chills of dread down into her core. Gathering up the children, she raced to the nearby home of Tom Walker,[50] an affluent farmer and a Blue Bill. She showed Walker the note, and he swiftly made arrangements for the woman and her children to take sanctuary 12 miles away at a home on Cosby Creek in nearby Cocke County. Walker sent an employee, George Sims, in a wagon to collect the Roses and their belongings and relocate them to Cosby Creek.

That was an all-day task, but when they arrived they were met with another bundle of withes and a note that said, "Laura Rose, you cannot live in this house." It had the same signature as the previous note.

Who knew the Rose family was headed there, and how could they have beaten them to the house? The hills had ears.

Obviously terrified, Sims reversed himself and returned to Walker with a fully loaded wagon. He told Walker what had happened and turned Laura Rose, her children and the wagon that contained them over to his boss. Though now late, Walker escorted them to the nearby home of Campbell Dugan, where they were allowed to spend the night.

The next day there was nowhere else to go except back to their own house, which is where Walker took them. But he awakened next morning to a bundle of withes on his own doorstep with a note warning him not to move the Roses again.

Walker was known to be hot-tempered. The note triggered a cussing fit and an oath that he would be ready for any White Cap assault that might come his way. Walker went to Sevierville and bought himself some ammunition and several sticks of dynamite.

A short time later another bundle arrived at the Rose home threatening 150 lashes if Laura Rose did not leave. The White Caps were

---

[50] Thomas Inman Walker, b. 22 AUG 1863, d. 16 DEC 1932, father of Cas Walker

upping the ante. Walker then moved them to a house in Sevierville that Dr. Henderson said she could use.

But when he got her to the house, there was another bunch of withes and a warning not to move her and the children in. Now Laura Rose was resigned to getting the beating the White Caps were promising. They were ordering her to leave but giving her no place to go. So she went home.

Every night brought the same fear, and every unidentifiable sound outside the home was a source of terror. Laura Rose began slipping out of her house at dusk and going to a different neighbor's home each night, begging to stay until morning. Then it caught up with her.

At the home of Frank Keeler one night, a group of about 10 masked men rode into the yard, knocked on the door and bum rushed those inside, dragging Laura Rose outside. She got her beating.

One man held her arms while another applied the switch. When he tired of his cruel task, he relinquished the withe to a comrade who took up where he left off. Finally, with Laura Rose lying unconscious on the ground, the White Caps rode away.

News of the whipping spread, and Tom Walker's temper got the best of him. He took their warning to heart, and believed they would be coming for him for having tried to help.

One night shortly after Laura's beating, three men wearing hoods rode into Walker's yard and demanded he come out. He did, but he went out the back door and down to the nearby creek under a bridge. That is where he had secured a Winchester shotgun and a battery which he planned to use to set off the explosives he had buried in the yard.

As the men entered the house, Walker's wife, Anna, grabbed an old shotgun and began attacking them with it. As they retreated into the yard, Walker set off the dynamite charges sending men and horses flying in all directions in the darkness. As they tried to flee across the bridge, Walker let go with a shotgun blast that separated one rider from his horse.

There is no documentation as to the extent of anyone's wounds that night, except the ones that got struck by Anna Walker's gun butt. But the riders did not get their revenge on Tom Walker.

Gun Battle at Dr. Henderson's Home on East Main Street

Dr. Henderson, by this time, was something of a marked man among the White Caps. It was common knowledge that he commanded and financed the Blue Bills, who were just as outside the law as the White Caps, but were facing no threat from the law and no scorn from any segment of the community—except the White Caps.

So the word spread among the White Caps that Henderson would feel the withe on his own back. If they could do it to him, logic told them, their supremacy as the county's enforcers would be cemented.

But good intelligence from an inside source has a way of trumping the best of battle plans, and so it was in this case, where the Blue Bills knew well ahead of time of the planned assault on Dr. Henderson. When the White Caps converged on the Henderson home, there was already a Blue Bill force in place and ready for action.

The informer rode up to the house *with* the attackers, but rode around back on arrival and linked up with his Blue Bill counterparts. Henderson was ordered out of his house, but he refused. That's when the shooting started and White Caps started dropping, screaming in pain.

When the gunfight was over, the Blue Bills stole away into the night, except for a few who remained to stand guard over the Henderson home.

It is said that there was a steady stream of wagons and buggies coming and going all night at the battle scene, carting off the dead and wounded.

The following morning all the casualties had been removed. How many were killed or wounded that night—or where in the hell law enforcement was during all this—remains a mystery. But there are claims that there were multiple suicides reported that next day, each body found with a pistol or shotgun nearby and a note that instructed wives how to raise their children.

In terms of lawlessness, in the late 1800s Sevier County was quite comparable to towns on the nation's storied frontier—but Dodge City's Wild West reputation was always overblown, and Tombstone was in a rocky wilderness that was not even a state yet and still referred to as a territory.

But Tombstone had its silver mines and Dodge City its cattle markets. Sevier County did not have anything like that. And it may have been that lack of a tangible, central commercial engine that created the environment that allowed Whitecapping to take root and flourish. There was little in the way of employment, and for many in the county every day may have been an exercise in what Thoreau called "quiet desperation"—just trying to make it until tomorrow or springtime or some relief date in the future. Perhaps White Cap activity was a depraved release valve for the frustration and aggression that was bound up in the day-to-day quest to eke out a hardscrabble existence.

None of that, of course, excuses it—or for that matter the actions of the Blue Bills—as a reasonable or justifiable response to the culture these individuals found themselves in. But it is likely a reflection of the largely unpolished character of a rural mountain enclave like Sevier County.

And the story was not over.

10

"Terrific Fight in a Sevier County Church"
Saturday, September 22, 1894

As the November off-year election approached, John Chiles Houk was running for re-election as the U.S. congressman in Tennessee's Second District.

Houk was a Knoxville lawyer who rose to his congressional seat on the tragic death of his father, Rep. Leonidas Campbell Houk, in May 1891. Congressman Leonidas C. Houk asked to have some medicine prepared for "nervousness" at DePue's Drugstore in Knoxville, and after he drank it he went to the front of the store and purchased a cigar. In the meantime, the druggist set a glass of arsenic on the counter, and when Congressman Houk went back to have more water he mistakenly drank the poison, and the attempts to save his life proved futile.[51] The younger Houk was re-elected in 1892, but two years later he was in a tough Republican primary battle to retain his seat with his father's former law partner, Henry R. Gibson.

On Friday night Houk campaigned in Jones Cove, then again at Emert's Cove at noon on Saturday, while on his way to give speech at the Baptist Church in Gatlinburg that evening. During his Friday night speech

---

[51] JUDGE HOUK DEAD, *Knoxville Daily Tribune*, May 26, 1891

Houk denounced Whitecapping, as "white-cappers had been doing a good deal of devilment in that section."[52] In 1894 one had to pass through Emert's Cove from Jones' Cove to get to Gatlinburg. It is interesting to note that Houk evidently spoke at Emert's Cove without provocation, perhaps due to the continued influence of the Emert's Cove Postmaster and Blue Bill, John Sam Springs.

Four alleged White Caps, Constable J. B. Trotter, Joe Trotter, Newton Trotter and Avery Cogsdell, arrived at the church ahead of Houk and declared that the Congressman should not speak there. They went so far as to "draw a dead line' between the church and a nearby schoolhouse, stating they would kill anyone who attempted to cross the line.

An old Veteran of the Union Army with both legs paralyzed approached the "dead line," and the four instigators told him they would kill him if he crossed the line. He dismissed them, telling them he didn't have much time left anyway, and he was going to the church. He was finally permitted to pass.

As Congressman Houk and his party arrived, the four instigators retreated inside the church. Houk stood his ground and gave his speech, but near the end Deputy Sheriff Sexton entered the church with a warrant for the arrest of one of the Trotter boys for threatening the Union Army Veteran.

And all hell broke loose.

Knives and guns were drawn, but no shots were fired and nobody was cut, and it seems most of the serious injuries were caused by rocks which were used as projectiles. Congressman Houk stood above the fray in the pulpit, nearly struck by an errant (or maybe not) rock. A skull was "crushed" and another had his cheek bone crushed.

---

[52] WET WITH BLOOD, *The Republican Leader*, September 27, 1894

It was reported that the floor in the center of the church was slippery with blood, and it finally ended when Deputy Sexton drew his pistols on the one for whom he had come to arrest.

We've included the article in its entirety, because we felt we couldn't render a distilled version of the event with enough detail to do it justice.

53

WET WITH BLOOD

Terrific Fight in a Sevier County Church,

WILL CAUSE TWO TO DIE

Four Toughs Tried to Prevent Houk From Speaking,

FLOOR SLIPPERY WITH BLOOD

All Over the Church the Fight Raged and Two Men Will Die From the Injuries Received — Four Shouters for Gibson Caused the Trouble.

Thos. W. Burke, of this city, returned this morning from Gatlinburg, Sevier county, and related to a Sentinel reporter the particulars of the double murder at a Houk meeting in that place Saturday night. Col. Burke says:

"On Friday night Congressman Houk spoke at Jones' Cove, and in the course of his speech denounced the whitecappers that have been doing a good deal of devilment in that section. He spoke about the outrages perpetrated by that organized gang in no uncertain terms, and while he won the appreciation of the law abiding citizens, he knew when he left there that he carried with him the enemity of the desperate gang that he had denounced.

"At noon Saturday he spoke to a large crowd at Emert's Cove, and from that place a cavalcade of old soldiers escorted him to Gatlinburg, seven miles away, where he was billed to speak at night.

---

53 WET WITH BLOOD, *The Republican Leader*, September 27, 1894

SCENE OF THE RIOT.

"The speech at Gatlinburg was to be made at the Baptist church, which had been thrown open for his use.

"Before the arrival of Congressman Houk and party, Constable J. B. Trotter, Joe Trotter, Newton Trotter, and Avery Cogsdell, suposed to be members of the whitecappers who had been denounced at Jones' cove, had reached the place and stated that Houk should not speak there. They went so far as midway between the church and the to

DRAW A DEAD LINE

school house near by, and declared they would kill any one attempting to cross that line to enter the church. The men were wild in their demeanor, and so excited and alarmed the citizens that about a score of ladies left the church, fearful of their lives, but fully as many more of the ladies remained.

"While the four desperadoes were making these demonstrations, an old ex-Federal soldier named Maples, whose legs are paralyzed from the knees down, started across the commons to the church. The four men yelled to him that if he crossed the dead line

THEY WOULD KILL HIM.

The old man replied, 'you can't rob me of many days, for I haven't long to live, and I'm going to that church or die in the attempt.' The old paralytic was, after some consultation, allowed to pass.

"As Congressman Houk and his party approached the church, they met the ladies who were retreating in terror from it, and learned the truth of the situation. The party pressed rapidly toward the church, and the quartette who had drawn the dead-line retreated, taking a position inside the building.

"Mr. Houk occupied the pulpit, and the church was crowded to its utmost capacity. When he arose to speak the four men I have mentioned before began lustily howling for Gibson, and for an hour the scene was a lively one. Finally Congressman Houk appealed to them to have some regard for the ladies present, for the men were using the most obscene and vulgar language.

"'Oh, G— d—n the ladies,' was the reply from one of the gang.

"'Then,' said Mr. Houk, 'if you have no regard for me or the ladies, have some respect for the house of God.'

"'G—d d—n the house of God,' the reply came, as vehemently as before.

"Mr. Houk then made the request that if any present didn't wish to hear him, they should retire. They met this suggestion with derision.

"It was then that Mr. Houk said he had come there to speak—that he meant business—that no gang of drunken toughs could bluff him away from an

68

engagement, and that he would either speak there or leave his dead body in the church.

THE DISTURBERS SILENCED.

"For a little while this appeared to silence the four disturbers, and Mr. Houk proceeded to deliver his address. He got along all right until he reached the last part of the speech. Just as he was saying 'in conclusion, ladies and gentlemen,'

THE ROW BEGAN.

"Deputy Sheriff Sexton had entered the church with a warrant for the arrest of one of the Trotter boys for threatening to shoot the old man Maples at the dead line. In anticipation of trouble Mr. Sexton had deputized about fifteen men in the crowd, to help him in case of an emergency. Sexton walked up to Trotter and read the warrant, beginning to read it about the time Mr. Houk was concluding the speech. Trotter resisted arrest and Sexton called to his deputies. The fight lasted about four or five minutes. Knives and pistols were drawn, but not a shot was fired and no one was cut. They fought up the center aisle to the altar and back again. Every man seemed to have a rock in his pocket, and the way these missiles flew through the church was a caution. Mr. Houk stood calmly in the pulpit and witnessed it all, while I stood by his side, and one big rock was thrown in such a manner as to pass behind us and nearly struck Mr. Houk on the head.

head.

THE FIRST TRAGEDY.

occurred in the rear of the church when Avery Cogsdale, the leader of the rioters, hit Redmond Maples on the head with a rock which he held in his hand, crushing Maples' skull in. Maples fell to the floor insensible and was carried from the church in a dying condition.

"Jim Compton, a strapping big young fellow, then struck Avery Cogsdale with his fist and knocked him over three benches. Cogsdale then crawled as far as the altar of the church when some unknown person hit him with something, crushing his cheek bone and the side of his head, and bursting an eye-ball. Cogsdale fell nearly at my feet, and I saw the person who hit him, but didn't know who it was.

"Others of the Trotter boys were about to renew the fight when Deputy Sheriff Sexton drew his pistols and covered the one for whom he had a warrant. That ended the fight. Avery Cogsdale was carried out in an unconscious condition and will probably die. Dr. Flennigan is attending their injuries, and told me he expected they are fatal in both cases.

"Of course there was no more speaking. The floor in the center of the church was slippery with blood. The windows of the church were knocked out by the rocks that had been thrown. Women had jumped from windows eight feet high to get out of the building. But Houk went there to speak and he did speak.

"I am satisfied," Col. Burke continued, that none of the citizens of Gatlinburg had anything to do with precipitating the row, and only those who were deputized by Mr. Sexton took part in quelling it."

11

The Gun Battle at Henderson Springs
October 25, 1894

S adly, in the time and place that defined the White Caps, Benjamin Farr might have been labeled as "uppity," but retrospectively, in this day and age, maybe "courageous" or an "activist."

The Civil War was nearly three decades in the past by 1894, and African Americans were "free" in the technical and legal sense. But to declare that they had assumed a full and equal presence in the American tapestry would be ludicrous. White society in the South was still a long way from accepting African Americans as full partners in the national experience.

However, the Fifteenth Amendment to the U.S. Constitution, ratified on Feb. 3, 1870, had given blacks—black men, that is—the right to vote.

Benjamin Farr, a black Sevier County resident who was described as mild-mannered, became vocal in his support for John Chiles Houk's re-election.

In Sevier County, the African American segment of the population was never significant enough in numbers to decide an election, let alone one in which Sevier was only one of several counties in the district.

Irrespective, "Uncle Ben" Farr had been out informally campaigning for Houk in a very public way and making eloquent speeches on the candidate's behalf.

During the run-up to the election, there had been a flurry of beatings in the area, and Farr awoke one evening to find his bed surrounded by White Caps. In an apparent response to his politicking, Farr endured not only a nighttime whipping but a humiliating addendum to his punishment. The White Caps forced him onto a stump and ordered him, "Now, damn you, make a speech for Gibson."

Fear now trumped Farr's politics, and he made the speech, after which the White Caps retreated.

Sometime during that same period, a woman named Ruth Massey, wife of James Massey and sister-in-law of Dr. Z. D. Massey, attracted the White Caps' glaring eyes for violating her marriage vows. Young and beautiful, she would probably have drawn their gaze even if her virtue had been intact.

But they did not believe that it was.

One night brought the battering down of the Masseys' door, and both husband and wife were forced outside in their nightclothes. James Massey was held by the White Caps at gunpoint while two others grabbed Ruth Massey's arms and forcibly wrapped them around a tree.

Her gown was lifted over her head and two other criminals applied the lash—in this case—buggy whips. They started at her feet and worked their way up. It was a brutal and horrific beating that ended after she cried out, "Let me down till I die!" And then she fainted.

She was carried back inside in the belief that she, too, had died from her ordeal. The White Caps fled, but Ruth Massey regained consciousness and survived.

As always, the neighbors were outraged, but not to the point of taking any action.

Whether in a bout with his conscience or with a bottle, a White Cap named William Brown let down his guard and told Uncle Ben Farr all about the Massey whipping. Brown also shared the organization's secrets and signs and the White Caps' intention to return to the home to attack James Massey. There was also a plan to converge on the home of Pink Rauhuff and either burn it down or blow it up.

Farr saw his chance to strike back at the men who had beaten and humiliated him, and he made certain Brown's information found its way to known White Cap opponents in the area.

On an October morning, a man named Elijah Helton came to Sevierville and told the newly elected Sheriff Millard Fillmore Maples about the planned attacks. Maples had won his post on a platform of combating the White Cap menace.[54]

But the sheriff told Helton that he had other pressing matters to attend to and could not personally participate in any law enforcement response to prevent the White Caps' actions—Chancery Court was in session, and his hands were full.

So Maples deputized Helton and another man, Mitchell F. Nichols, and instructed them to gather all the sympathizers they could find to prevent the attacks.

On October 25, 1894, Helton and his band gathered at Henderson Springs, a short distance from the mill at Pigeon Forge. They put together a plan for their evening's work and started for the Massey home.

About a half-mile from Henderson Springs a bluff overlooks the Little Pigeon River. The road got narrow there, and Helton and Nichols were riding along there, accompanied by William A. Henderson, Ash W. Nichols, M. V. Lewellen, John Myers and Pink Rauhuff.

---

[54] Millard Fillmore Maples was High Sheriff of Sevier County from 1894-1898

Ash Nichols and Pink Rauhuff had positioned themselves a few hundred yards down the river, watching the road for suspicious travelers.

Enroute to the Massey home, Henderson, Myers and Mitchell Nichols got slightly ahead of the others in their party and were the first to encounter four unmasked men coming from the other direction, who hid their faces behind the brims of their hats as they rode by.

It was suspicious to meet riders there at that time of day, but since they wore no disguises there was no reason to detain them. Seconds later as the mystery men met Helton and Lewellen, angry words interrupted the rhythm of hoof beats.

That was followed by pistol shots. The first bullet from a White Cap pistol struck Lewellen in the chest, taking him to the ground.

Helton raised a double-barrel shotgun and emptied it, removing two White Caps from the fight. But as he reloaded, a White Cap named James Gibson rushed up and fired twice, both bullets striking Helton in the head.

Ash Nichols and Rauhuff, hearing the gunfire, wheeled their horses around and galloped to the scene, where they found the bodies of Helton and White Cap Isaac Keeble. Labe Latham of the White Cap contingent was also on the cold ground, gasping and moaning. Not knowing if they were in the middle of a crossfire, Rauhuff and Nichols retreated the way they had come.

Lewellen, agonizing from his chest wound, headed home.

Mitchell Nichols and William Henderson left the main road, went around the foot of the bluff and forded the river in chest-deep water. All the time they could hear the anguished cries from the killing ground.

It was Latham, crying, "Oh, God I'm shot, and I'm dying. Friends, please come help me."

Mitchell Nichols thought he recognized the moaning voice as that of his brother, Ash. He went to a spot directly across the river from the scene and listened again.

"Oh, Jim, where are you? I am shot and bleeding to death," came the painful plea.

Nichols and Henderson decided the voice did not belong to anyone in their troupe, and they went home.

There, Mitchell Nichols found out that his brother had not returned from the fight, and that rekindled his anguish all over again.

He paced the floor late into the night, saying, "Oh, my God! The poor unfortunate man is dying all alone by the riverside. Surely it must be brother Ash."

When he could not stand it anymore he returned to a point near the scene to listen. But now there was silence, broken only by the hoot of an owl. Latham was dead, too.

What Mitchell could not know was that Ash was at the home of Rauhuff, fearing that one of the fatalities of the gunfight was Mitchell.

People arriving at the killing scene the next day discovered a sack beneath Keeble's body that contained White Cap masks.

Again, tensions rose to the boiling point in the area, and longtime friendships crumbled.

Uncle Ben Farr's friend, William Brown, and two others turned state's evidence in the case, resulting in the arrests of Dan Davis, the alleged leader of the White Cap group, and 10 comrades, all charged with the beatings of Ruth Massey and Farr.

All went before a justice of the peace and posted bond, but two White Caps were on the grand jury that considered their cases, and no indictments were returned. They all went free.

The record appears incomplete on whether James Gibson ever faced charges in the killing of Helton, who was at the time technically a sheriff's deputy.

Lewellen died a year after the battle, the bullet wound to his chest blamed for ultimately killing him.

KU KLUX KLAN

Sevier County Terrorized by Bands of Outlaws.

THREE CITIZENS FOUND DEAD

Terrible Battle Between the White-caps and the "Blue Bills."

A GANG OF BLOODY DEVILS

Homes of Courtesans Where Murders Often Occurred.

Deplorable Deviltries Arouse a Fever Heat of Excitement Near Sevierville.

Special to The Chattanooga Times.

Knoxville, Oct. 26.—Whitecapism and outlawry is rampant in Sevier county and as a result the bodies of three citizens were found lying dead on a bluff near Henderson Springs yesterday morning. Their names are Laban Latham, Lige Helton and another by the name of Kibble.

Excitement is at fever heat and a most deplorable condition of affairs seems to exist. The following particulars were given by one of the most reputable citizens of Sevierville tonight:

Thursday it was learned that a band of whitecaps had determined to visit the house of a disreputable woman back of a bluff on Pigeon river, and administer a severe whipping to the occupants of the house.

The continuous outrages of the organization have resulted in the recent organization of an anti-white cap secret order, whose members call themselves "Blue Bills." The latter heard of the

Proposed Whipping Expedition

of the whitecaps near Henderson Springs, and a crowd of them armed themselves and went out to see that the whipping was not done. The evidence yesterday morning was substantial and horrifying enough to know that the two opposing orders met and had a fight.

Lathman and Kibble are of the whitecaps, and Helton is a "Blue Bill." It is known that the two parties met on the top of the bluff between 8 and 9 o'clock Thursday night and a heavy firing was opened. Whether the "Blue Bills" laid in ambush and opened fire or whether they were ambushed by the whitecaps seems to be a mooted question. Nor can it be definitely ascertained how many were on each side, but it is supposed that there were ten or twelve.

The people of that vicinity are terrorized, and so much so that they will not come up and volunteer information and thus assist in bringing about speedy justice to the offenders of law and order. Sheriff Maples recently imported a couple of fine bloodhounds, but he was afraid to turn them on the trail for the reason that there are so many of both orders who would be only too glad to

Shoot the Dogs Down.

The sheriff took these dogs through Knoxville a couple of weeks ago, and they were admired by several people here. The sheriff has sworn in extra deputies and is making every effort to apprehend the guilty parties.

Ever since the war Sevier county has had more or less experience with white-caps. Prior to about three years they had become quieted down so long that the reputable citizens of the county felt they were rid of them. About three years ago the whitecap business was revived, for the purpose mainly of ridding certain localities of disreputable women. These women had taken up their abodes in the mountains and in various parts of the county, and their homes were the scenes of brawls and fights and often murder and were veritable traps of the devil to ruin young men. The officers of the county arrested numbers of them and they were brought into court, tried and were fined and their friends would promptly step up and pay the fines and the women would promptly take up their old abodes again.

The decent people became incensed and finding the power of the court was limited, some of them decided on holding

A Few Whipping Bees

and see what effect that would have. These were not whitecaps nor any secret order further than to set a few examples with the hope that the rest would take a hint. However, they were called white-caps, and their conduct seemed to give license to unprincipled characters to organize also.

Soon the law and order element became superseded by the worst gang of devils that ever infested this part of the state and their deviltment was visited upon those who had anything to do with trying to drive out these bad women.

Nearly every good barn in the county has been burned, to say nothing of the heavy losses by the burning of their contents. They became so bold at one time that barns were set on fire in broad day light and an instance is cited where one of these women was caught setting fire to a barn stored full of baled hay. Thus the righteous but unlawful conduct of good citizens in time became a curse to the county and this triple murder is one of the fruits thereof.

It is barely possible that other lives have been lost in this battle in the dark. Parties who heard the shooting say that there was enough of it to have wiped out a regiment had it been properly applied.

The scene of the shooting is on a high wooded bluff on Pigeon river, about four and a half miles from Sevierville, and one-half mile from Henderson Springs. More trouble is anticipated, for a strong feeling is being aroused to wipe out outlawry from the county, if all the decent people have to take up arms to do it.

Associated Press Account.

Washington, Oct. 25.—A special from Knoxville, Tenn., says:

For two years there has existed in Sevier county a large organization of white-caps. They have committed many outrages on defenseless citizens, especially women and colored people. Some weeks ago another gang was organized in opposition which is known as "Blue Bills." Last night a body of whitecaps started out to do a man who lives five miles from Sevierville. It happened that this man was a "Blue Bill," and he hastily summoned his gang together. About twenty of them secreted themselves in a dense thicket of laurel. Shortly before midnight they heard the approach of the whitecaps. As they approached the thicket the "Blue Bills" opened fire with Winchesters, and a pitched battle raged for several minutes. Two whitecaps, Laban Latham and John Kibble, were killed and several others injured. The "Blue Bills" lost one man. Elishan Allen, a prominent farmer, and two or three others of their clique were badly wounded.

THREE MEN DEAD.

Midnight Battle in Sevier County Between White Caps and Blue Bills.

Latter Recently Organized to Exterminate the Bloody White Caps.

Masked Men Start out to Whip a Defenceless Woman and Meet A Band of Well Armed Blue Bills.

Whitecapism and outlawry is certainly rampant in Sevier County and as a result the bodies of three citizens were found lying dead on a bluff near Henderson Springs yesterday morning.

Their names are Laban Latham, Lige Helton and another by the name of Kibble.

Excitement is at fever heat and a most deplorable condition of affairs seem to exist.

The following particulars were given by one of the most reputable citizens of Sevierville:

Thursday it was learned that a band of white caps had determined to visit the house of a disreputable woman back of a bluff on Pigeon river, about half a mile from Henderson Springs, and administer a severe whipping to the occupants of the house.

The continuous outrages of this organization has resulted in the recent organization of a band of "Blue Bills." The latter heard of the proposed whipping expedition of the white caps near Henderson Springs and a crowd of them armed themselves and went out to see that the wipping was not done.

The evidence yesterday morning was substantial and horrifying enough to know that the two opposing orders met and had a fight.

Latham and Kibble are of the white-caps and Helton is a "Blue Bill."

It is known that the two parties met on the top of the bluff between eight and nine o'clock Thursday night and a heavy firing was opened.

Whether the Blue Bills laid in ambush and opened fire, or whether they were ambushed by the whitecaps seems to be a mooted question. Nor can it be definitely ascertained how many were on each side, but it is supposed that there were ten or twelve on a side.

The people of that vicinity are terrorized and so much so that they will not come up and volunteer information and thus assist in bringing about speedy justice to the offenders of law and order.

Sheriff Maples recently imported a couple of fine blood hounds but he was afraid to turn them on the trail for the reason that there are so many of both orders, who would be only too glad to shoot the dogs down.

The sheriff took these dogs through Knoxville a couple of weeks ago and they were admired by several people here.

He sent a request to the Journal to say nothing about them as he wanted to use them before the whitecaps had learned he had them. However it was soon known throughout the mountains that he had the hounds and no doubt the whitecaps have sworn to shoot the dogs on sight for the good of the order.

The sheriff has sworn in extra deputies and is making every effort to apprehend the guilty parties.

Ever since the war Sevier county has had more or less experience with white caps. Prior to about three years ago, so says an old Sevier county citizen, they had become quieted down so long that the reputable citizens of the county felt they were rid of them.

About three years ago the whitecap business was revived for the purpose, mainly of ridding certain localities of disreputable women. These women had taken up their abodes in the mountains and in various parts of the county, and their homes were the scenes of brawls and fights and often murder and were veritable traps of the devil to ruin young men.

The officers of the county arrested numbers of them and they were brought into court, were tried and were fined and their friends would promptly step up and pay the fines and the women would promptly take up their old abodes again.

The decent people became incensed and finding the powers of the court was limited, some of them decided on holding a few whipping bees and see what effect that would have. These were not whitecaps nor any secret order further than to set a few examples with the hope that the rest would take a hint.

However they were called whitecaps and their conduct seemed to give license to unprincipled characters to organize also.

Soon the law and order element became superceded by the worst gang of devils that ever infested this part of the state and their devilment was visited upon those who had anything to do with trying to drive out these bad women.

As one man up that way said, within the past three years nearly every good barn in the county had been burned, to say nothing of the heavy losses by the burning of their contents.

They became so bold at one time that barns were set on fire in broad day light and an instance is cited where one of these women was caught setting fire to a barn stowed full of bailed hay.

Thus the righteous but unlawful conduct of good citizens in time became a curse to the county and this triple murder is one of the fruits thereof.

It is barely possible that other lives have been lost in this battle in the dark The Journal's informant was on the scene of the fight but could not learn whether any had been wounded seriously or otherwise.

Parties who heard the shooting say that there was enough of it to have wiped out a regiment had it been properly applied.

The scene of the shooting was on a high wooded bluff on the Pigeon river, about four and one half miles from Sevierville and one half mile from Henderson Springs.

Of course more trouble is anticipated for a strong feeling is being aroused to wipe outlawry from the country If all decent people have to take up arms to do it.

About a month later the White Caps/Blue Bills saga took another turn. It was not a good one.

The Murder of Dr. James Aron Henderson
November 30, 1894

Thirty-six days after the shootout at Henderson Springs, as the evenings were getting chillier, Dr. James Henderson and his second wife, the former Lauretta Murphy, were chatting by their fireside with a neighbor, W. A. Green. It was a Friday evening—the sun sets early in late November, and even Main Street in Sevierville was dark and devoid of people. That is what allowed the man with the shotgun to slip up to the doctor's window without anyone noticing.

He could see the three through the open blinds, their faces a warm orange in the firelight as they talked and chuckled. Slowly he raised his weapon, training it on the doctor. From that distance, it was hard to miss with a shotgun.

The man squeezed the trigger.

One second Henderson was talking to his friend, and the next his face was shredded by a shotgun blast that no one saw coming. It was a gruesome scene, the doctor dying as he heard the shot.

A jury of inquest, assembled by A.T. Atchley, the county's coroner, readily identified William H. "Bill" Gass as the killer. A warrant was sworn out, and Gass was arrested and jailed under heavy guard.

Dr. Henderson's brother, District Attorney General George Mac Henderson, arrived in Sevierville in a day or so with a casket that he had purchased in Knoxville. George Henderson publicly disputed the coroner's findings, saying he believed his brother had many enemies and that the murder was likely another White Cap atrocity.

A logical conclusion, but not this time. The headlines told the story:

HAD RUINED HIS WIFE.

Terrible Tragedy in the Quiet Town of Sevierville Last Night.

Dr. J. A. Henderson, a Prominent Physician, Killed in His Bed.

W. H. Gass, Whose Wife He Ruined, Supposed to Have Fired the Shot.

Sickening Details of the Unfortunate Affair.

Sequel to a Trip to Knoxville by the Murdered Man and the Now Sad and Repentant Woman.

HEAD SHOT OFF

Dr. J. A. Henderson Was Foully Assassinated While in His Home at Sevierville Last Night.

DEED CHARGED TO W. H. GASS

Mrs. Gass Confessed to Having Spent Some Time in Knoxville With Dr. Henderson.

GUILT IS NOT YET SETTLED

Attorney General Henderson Says a Man Named Taylor May Have Murdered His Brother.

Bill Gass had eloped to Knoxville with Julia Lillian "Lille" Maples when the bride was but a16-year-old beauty.

On Friday, Nov. 30, 1894, Knoxville Journal breathlessly reported:

> "Last Sunday afternoon a young man of perhaps 35, of medium build, and wearing a light mustache, appeared before the desk of the Hotel Imperial in the city and taking up a pen registered in a bold hand:
>
> "Ella Jones, Rutledge"
>
> "J.A. Henderson, Sevierville"
>
> "Miss Jones, who had gone to the ladies' parlor, was assigned to room 64, and Dr. Henderson was given room 83, which is located on the fourth floor. That night the couple appeared together at supper, and everyone in the dining room was attracted to the young woman's beauty. She appeared to be about 20, with large, lustrous black eyes, arched brows, black hair and cheeks as red and rosy as a ripe peach. She was of medium height and attired in a plain black dress that perfectly fitted her well rounded figure."

Miss Jones was actually Lillie Maples Gass, who was having an extramarital affair with Dr. Henderson. Rumors about his wife's unfaithfulness finally got back to Gass, and he conducted his own investigation.

Gass accused his young wife of the adultery, and she broke down weeping and admitted her indiscretion with Dr. Henderson at the Hotel Imperial, where a newspaper advertisement showed rooms costing $2.50 a night.

So Gass, as a wronged husband, had a motive for the high-profile killing. For his own safety, he was held in a Knoxville jail until his Sevierville trial, at which he was found not guilty. The reasons for the acquittal may have come from sympathy for a man betrayed or because there were White Caps on the jury.

Lillie Maples Gass, by the way, was the only daughter of Sheriff M.F. Maples, who had been vehemently opposed to the marriage.

1894 also produced one other consequential event in the White Cap saga in Sevier County—Sheriff Maples kept a campaign promise and hired a new deputy named Thomas "Tom" Houston Davis.

12

The Killing of Ellen Jane (Sallie) Deats

We essentially entered into a contract with you at the beginning of this book, that we would endeavor to tell the story of the White Caps in Sevier County as truthfully and thoroughly as we possibly could. We also said White Capping, unlike a lot of other similar "Night Riders" organizations was not a racially motivated response to deviance within a community.

Then we came across the Ellen Jane (Sallie) Deats killing, and it gave us a moment of pause. She was originally referred to as Sallie Deats, but the state was able prove her name was actually Ellen Jane Deats, but not before Knox County Sheriff Groner received a letter from Hickory, North Carolina dated January 19, 1895, from O. C. Deitz. Mr. Deitz believed that the deceased woman was his sister, and wanted to know where her children were.[57] We did not find any other articles suggesting the deceased was Mr. Deitz's sister.

Was the Ellen Deats killing racially motivated? And if so, was it a premeditated White Cap racially motivated hate crime? Or, was it simply

---

[57] SALLIE DEATS' NAME, *Knoxville Sentinel*, Knoxville, TN, February 20, 1895

another crime where there was a pre-exiting connection to the White Caps, and because that was the case, it was labeled a White Cap crime? Or connecting White Caps to the crime could have been what newspapers have done ever since Joseph Pulitzer and William Randolph Hearst competed with one another in the later 1800s—sensationalizing stories to sell newspapers.

We don't know, so we're going to present the information we discovered and let you come to your own conclusions.

Interestingly enough, you'll not find the name Ellen Jane (Sallie) Deats in the Crozier book, the Cas Walker book, the Eyes of Midnight or Cummings' thesis, but the killing and subsequent trials were highly publicized in the Knoxville newspapers.

Ellen Deats, reportedly "a woman of ill repute,"[58] lived seven miles from Knoxville, on the Sevierville Pike, near the Lige Dunn farm. It was reported she was "the mother of four children, two of whom are negroes, their father being the negro who owned the property on which the woman lived."[59]

Another article from the Knoxville Evening Sentinel on Monday, January 14, 1895, states that Ellen Deats lived on Sevierville Road, about six miles from Knoxville, and "had two white children and one colored."[60] It was reported that some people had been in the habit of shouting "Sambo" as they passed by her house, to aggravate her, and that she would sometimes shoot at the transgressors from her window.

On the evening of Wednesday, January 2, 1895, four men passed by Ellen Deats' house: Sam Jenkins, Zeb (aka Jep or Jap) Jenkins, Jim Ellis

---

[58] IN THE NECK, *The Chattanooga Daily Times*, Chattanooga, Tennessee, Saturday, January 5, 1895
[59] ibid
[60] SOMEONE SHOUTED SAMBO, *The Evening Sentinel*, Knoxville, Tennessee, Monday, January 14, 1895

and Joe Parton. All four were reputedly White Caps.[61] By their own admission they had been drinking, and the reports about how the killing unfolded varied from the initial reporting through the end of the trials.

According to one report, some of the men had visited the South Knoxville livery stables of Joe Jones and his son, where they had a few drinks. It was alleged that the men were overheard at the livery planning to *visit* the Deats woman, and if she didn't "permit them to *visit* her they would do her up."[62] This eyewitness testimony seems to support the claim that she was of ill-repute. Whether she was or not, she would have attracted the attention of any White Caps who still believed it was their mission to correct perceived breaches of community behavioral standards. The article goes on to say:

> "And the presumption is that inasmuch as she had some two weeks previous fired a shot at one of their friends who called at her house in a boisterous way they had decided to give her a good whipping, a la white cap, possibly by order of that gang. It is the usual way of proceeding in Sevier County.
>
> Their woman whipping policy is notorious. In fact they are not a whit better than the ancient Cherokee Indians. They burn down houses and barns, and shoot women very much in the manner of early barbarians.
>
> They have come to place little value on human life and it is quite the thing to have a record for killing some one, no matter how cowardly it was done."[63]

---

[61] LEADER OF THE WHITE CAPS, *The Journal and Tribune*, Knoxville, Tennessee, Monday, January 7, 1895
[62] LEADER OF THE WHITE CAPS, January 7, 1895
[63] Ibid

It was reported that when they threw empty whiskey bottles against the door and asked for admission they were refused. This enraged the men and someone opened fire on the house with a pistol—four shots were allegedly directed at the house, and the woman returned fire with a shotgun. The men eventually realized the woman had been shot in the neck, and fled.

A witness reported that "he heard loud boisterous talk, which was followed by three shots. Directly afterward four men, two on each horse and riding a gray and sorrel horse, passed his house at a rapid gait."[64]

Eventually all four men, Sam and Jap Jenkins, Joe Parton and James Ellis, were tried—Jap Jenkins, Joe Parton and James Ellis were acquitted. Sam Jenkins fled to the mountains and was in hiding for several months, and eventually turned himself in and was tried and convicted.[65] Eyewitness testimony from Etta Reed offers a glimpse into the Deats' home during and after the exchange of gunfire:

"She lived with her three children—oldest about thirteen years old; a girl. Remember night of shooting. It occurred between six and seven, after dark. (Explains location.) First thing I heard was shooting. Was going in my front room. Went to front window. Saw flash of pistol twice on outside of Deats house. They were quick. Could tell that persons who fired were on outside. Couldn't hear anybody talking. Couldn't see anyone. Then saw a flash from house and heard report. Am positive it was after the two shots on the outside. Then heard one from road. Can't locate. Only had time to step from window to door between first two and last shot. We went over there. Found Mrs. Deats lying near the fireplace. Had a talk with her. We laid her on the bed. We asked if she was shot and she said she felt awful

---

[64] QUICKLY OVERTAKEN, *Knoxville Journal and Tribune*, January 9, 1895
[65] MURDER CHARGED, *The Journal and Tribune*, May 30, 1896

bad, and wanted a doctor, and asked me to pray for her children that she hadn't lied right."

Those are the facts of the case, as best we could determine them. By all accounts all four defendants had been drinking heavily that day, and it had been somewhat customary to harass the Deats woman, for whatever reason. But it seems unlikely that at its core it was a racially motivated Whitecapping incident, and more likely that it was four men, under the influence of alcohol and with Whitecap ties, who made a series of bad decisions that led to a woman dying needlessly.

13

Til Death Do Us Part:
Sheriff Maples & Squire Wynn

On Saturday night, April 27, 1895, a band of White Caps gathered at the home of a man named Jerry Woodsby, who lived in a cabin on property owned by James Catlett, the patriarch of a prominent family in Sevier County. Woodsby had been employed to work on Catlett's farm but had quit for unknown reasons. As previously cited in the Cummings thesis, these events are related to the use of Whitecapping methods by landowners as a means of controlling tenant farmers or sharecroppers.

The evening stillness was disturbed by a band of White Caps, who surrounded Woodsby's cabin and demanded he come to the door. After Woodsby refused, the bandits battered down the door with a fence rail and dragged him outside, where he received one of the White Caps' fearsome whippings. The beating ended with a stern demand to go back to work for Catlett or face another, and even more brutal whipping the next time. Woodsby was bloodied and led back inside.

Their dastardly deeds were not finished on this evening and Tom Gibson, unlike most others in the county, did not keep a firearm in the house. Apparently he never needed one, or could not afford one.

Old Tom Gibson was an uncomplicated man, a live-and-let-live sort for whom springs, summers and autumns were seasons of hard labor and winters were to be endured and merely survived. There was nothing particularly easy about Gibson's hardscrabble existence. He did not have much, but he seemed to have what he needed, and pretty much all he asked of life was a peaceful homestead near Sevierville with his wife and his daughter Callie.

And biscuits on Sunday morning; he liked that, too.

Callie had helped make her hard-working father's life a little easier with her care and support, however one newspaper article stated, "she does not bear the best character and is the mother of a child."[66] A young mother with a child born out of wedlock would have gotten the unwanted attention of the White Caps, and this would have been enough for them to pay the Gibson house a visit.

Gibson was in Sevierville getting some provisions earlier that evening, April 27, 1895, among them a sack of flour.

"I'll have biscuit for breakfast Sunday morning," he told those he met.[67]

It would not happen.

The White Caps beat down Gibson's door and stepped inside, while stating their intention to give Callie Gibson a whipping for her moral shortcomings. According to the newspaper reports only Gibson and Callie were home that evening.

Tom Gibson surely must have known he was overmatched, yet his fatherly instincts took over, and Old Tom counterattacked with the only weapon he could get his hands on. Gibson rose and rushed the White Cap

---

[66] ASSASSINATED, *The Knoxville Tribune*, April 29, 1895
[67] Crozier, 93

leader with his chair, while Callie fled out a rear door. Callie Gibson would have heard the blasts from the double-barrel shotgun as she ran away, with full knowledge of what it meant for Old Tom and how futile their efforts to alter that outcome would have been. So she kept on running in the darkness toward refuge in another neighbor's home.

The first shotgun blast missed, but the second one found its mark. Old Tom took the shotgun's full fury in his chest, the sixty-three shot removed by a physician likely killed him before he hit the cabin floor. Their mission having gone south in a rapid and deadly fashion, the nameless White Caps dissolved into the night. Old Tom lay dead on the cabin floor until morning.

News of Gibson's death did not take long to complete the two-mile journey to Sevierville, bringing Sheriff Maples, Dr. Massengill, Dr. Walker, Judge Houk and a crowd to the cabin.[68] Something approaching disbelief was the most common reaction to the killing, followed by rising rage that permeated the community.

Maples vowed to run the killers to ground, and appealed to William Wynn to loan the sheriff his bloodhounds to track the murderers. Wynn refused not only the use of his dogs for the chase, but also declined to participate himself as part of a posse.

Whether that raised any alarm in the sheriff's mind cannot be known, and it would not be the last time that Sheriff Maples and William Wynn butted heads—but there would be a last time.

The Gibson murder and subsequent refusal of William Wynn to cooperate with or participate in the manhunt prompted the sheriff to appear before the County Court a month later and request $150 to purchase bloodhounds for use in future pursuits.[69] The County Court, made up of Justices of the Peace—some of whom were likely White Caps—hotly debated buying the dogs, but they seemed disinclined to do

---

[68] Crozier, 95
[69] Cummings, 70

so until they got a supporting argument from a sheriff's deputy with a sharp sense of logic and a persuasive tongue.

"This court has just appropriated a large sum of money," Tom Davis said, "to build a new courthouse. Crime after crime is being committed by a band of White Caps, and to invest a small sum of money in a pair of bloodhounds to run them down, and thus regain the good name of Sevier County, would be of vastly more importance to the county than a new courthouse to try them in."[70]

Davis's argument swung enough votes, twenty-one in favor and eight opposed, and the money was appropriated. But shortly thereafter a lawsuit was filed in Chancery Court to block the appropriation.[71]

> "Before the money could be drawn, however, a friend of Wynn's, Jesse Atchley, prevented the purchase by filing an injunction with the chancery court. Atchley argued that the appropriation had been made illegally. The court granted the injunction and five months later ruled in favor of the plaintiffs."

By then the outrage over Old Tom Gibson's murder had died down, the county never bought the bloodhounds, and Gibson's killers never faced a courtroom.

The period between late fall 1894 and the spring of 1895 was a tipping point in the White Caps of Sevier County saga: the assembly of the mechanism by which the White Caps would eventually be eradicated from Sevier County had already begun when Millard Filmore Maples had been elected High Sheriff in 1894; the Battle of Henderson Springs had demonstrated that a vigilante solution to a vigilante problem was not the answer; the murder of the Blue Bills' de facto leader, Dr. Henderson, hastened the aforementioned ineffectiveness of the Blue Bills; and the

[70] Crozier, 95
[71] Cummings, 70

political leadership in Knox County grew increasingly uneasy about the wanton lawlessness and corrupt legal system in their next door neighbor.

As a result, the conditions were right for a small scale revolution, an overthrow of the status quo, so that the White Cap-prominent landowner-Justices of the Peace coalition could be decisively and irreversibly defeated.

A couple of twists of the fateful kaleidoscope later—a series of inciting incidents and the willingness of Sheriff Maples and Deputy Sheriff Davis to seek help from their friends and acquaintances in Knoxville—and the beginning of the end started to unfold.

14

Endgame Crime Spree
July-December 1896

The Ambush of Aaron McGill
July 1896

Aaron McGill, alias McMahan, lived in the splendor of Wears Valley—a gorgeous basin surrounded by mountains. Pigeon Forge lies North/northeast of Wear's Valley, through a couple of narrow passes into another valley that is home to the Pigeon River. Reports say that the Pigeon Forge area had more White Caps than any other part of Sevier County.

At age 44, McGill was a successful farmer. He had married Caroline Green on March 2, 1868, and they had a large number of children, some old enough to have children of their own. His youngest was still an infant.

McGill's daughter, Mary, was married to James Clabough, a man of modest means but respectability, who lived in Little Cove. Mary had been accused by the White Caps of not being virtuous, so they visited her and administered a merciless whipping.

Two of the White Caps who called upon Mary Clabough, Newt Green and West Hendricks, were first cousins of hers. Mary's mother, Caroline, was a sister of both Green's father and Hendricks' mother.

Bayard Yadon tells it like this, from the June 2, 1929, Knoxville News Sentinel:

"In the absence of her husband, the manuscript says, Green and Hendricks, her cousins, "visited her, grossly insulted her and ordered her to get dinner." Armed with a butcher knife, she drove them from her house. They threatened her with the White-Caps. She treated the matter lightly."

"Perhaps you don't know by what authority we speak," said Hendricks.

"Oh, yes I do," came the tart reply. "I've seen your cowardly 'Graveyard Hosts' pass up and down the road at all hours of the night.

"Well, you're liable to see us tonight," Hendricks warned, as they departed.

That night her home was surrounded by the "Graveyard Hosts." Her door was battered down. The White-Caps dragged her from her bed, in her night clothes, and unmercifully whipped her. She fought like a tigress but was powerless in the hands of the white-robed demons.

Her father, Aaron McGill, was there early next morning—saw her huddled in bed with blood-soaked garments sticking to her back.

Then she told him of Green and Hendricks' visit the day before and their insults.

To say that he was enraged falls far short of expressing his emotion. He was furious, a veritable storm of vengeance.

In this frame of mind, he departed. Around the bend in the road he met Green and Hendricks. With a roar like that of a lion he charged his two enemies.

The fight was cast and furious. Every time Aaron shot out his long, muscular arm, one of the White-Caps went down. The assailants of his daughter were soon beaten. With the blood oozing through their garments, Aaron left them in the road.

At a justice of the peace trial on the following day—a proceeding attended by scores of unrobed White-Caps— McMahan was acquitted. But the hooded legions were not finished."[72]

The next day, Wednesday, July 15, 1896, McGill, Clabough and McGill's son, Amos, went to Pigeon Forge in a two-horse wagon loaded with wheat to be milled. While at the mill, a group identified as White Caps encountered the McGills and Clabough and became engaged in a heated verbal confrontation over the whipping.

Toward mid-afternoon, the three men began the arduous trip back from the mill to Wears Valley. Four o'clock found them passing through Little Cove at a point where there are deep woods and steep ravines on the edges of the road. As they rattled down the road Aaron McGill heard a noise from the forest and turned to see Hendricks and Green open fire on them. The horses were spooked and began to run. Aaron McGill grievously wounded, was unable to stop them. Clabough was wounded in the back of the neck and dazed, falling unconscious from the wagon. Amos McGill took a bullet to the leg.

Passersby managed to halt and calm the horses and took the wounded men to the nearby home of John Myers. As always, members of the

[72] Bayard Yadon, Unmasking the Sevier County 'White-Caps', *The Knoxville News-Sentinel*, June 2, 1929

surrounding area rushed to the Myers home, as did Dr. Z. D. Massey, who tended all three men's wounds.

SEVIER COUNTY TRAGEDY.

Two Suspects Bound to Court For Saturday's Shooting.

As reported exclusively in The Journal yesterday there was a fracus in Sevier county this week in which Aaron Mc-Gill, Amos McGill and James Clabor were shot from ambush the shooting occurring Wednesday morning between Wear's valley and Pigeon Forge. West Hendricks and Newt Green were arrested as suspects and Thursday afternoon at 2 o'clock were tried before Squire Tarwater and Squire Dryan and were bound to court. Neither gave bond and both were locked up in the Sevierville jail yesterday morning. There is considerable bitterness on both sides but it is hoped that there will be no further violence. The three wounded men are yet living but Aaron McGill may die at any time.

The Journal and Tribune,
Knoxville, Tennessee,
Saturday, July 25, 1896

TWO MAY DIE.

Bloody Shooting Affray in Little Cove, Sevier County.

How the Affair Occurred and What Caused It. Suspected Shootists Have Been Arrested.

Special to The Journal.

Sevierville, Tenn., July 23.—As the result of a shooting scrape that occurred in Little Cove last Wednesday two men lie at the point of death and a third is painfully wounded. The men are James Clabor, Aaron McGill alias McMahon and his son, Amos McGill.

The fuss that culminated in the shooting originated as follows:

Last week Joe Hendricks reported to the white caps that James Clabor and his wife were disreputable characters. Last Friday night the white caps visited the Clabor home and gave Clabor and his wife a hundred licks each.

On Monday Clabor assembled his friends, among them being the two Mc-Gills and proceeded to the Hendricks place. The crowd met Joe Hendricks and gave him a severe thrashing. He immediately swore out warrants for his assailants and they were tried on Tuesday before Squire Tarwater of Wear's Valley. They were discharged and it is rumored that the terror in which they are held by the community and the fear of bodily harm from them influenced the court more than the innocence of defendants.

Wednesday morning Clabor and the two McGills made a trip from Wear's Valley to Pigeon Forge in a wagon. In the afternoon they started on their return and when about half way and while passing through what is known as Little Cove, several shots were fired from the bushes by the side of the road and the men in the wagon fell over very badly wounded.

The shooting occurred not far from a house and the wounded men were taken there and their wounds dressed.

Aaron McGill is the most seriously wounded and is probably dead by this time. He was shot through the body from one side to the other and also in the face. James Clabor was shot through the neck and his left arm was shattered by a bullet. Amos McGill received a bullet through his leg.

Immediately after the shooting Aaron McGill's affidavit was taken to the effect that Newton Green and West Hendricks were the assailants. These two were arrested Wednesday night and were to have had a preliminary hearing in Wear's Valley yesterday.

Messrs. Penland and Zirkle have been retained by the defendants and a hot fight will be made to clear them.

The Journal and Tribune,
Knoxville, Tennessee,
Friday, July 24, 1896

99

Aaron McGill spent 10 days in agony before dying, but during that time he insisted multiple times that Green and Hendricks fired the bullets that downed all three men. His firm accusation never wavered. Amos McGill and Clabough both survived their wounds. Others also said they had seen Green and Hendricks in possession of firearms near where the shootings took place. The two were arrested shortly after the shootings by Sheriff Maples and Deputy R. C. McGill and were bound over to a grand jury on high bond on charges of felonious assault. After Aaron McGill died, the charge was modified to murder and their bond was revoked. They remained in the Sevier County jail for seven months, awaiting the March 1897 term of court before going on trial.

Both were convicted of murder, but while they were incarcerated awaiting action on their appeals in the case, Green and Hendricks joined other prisoners in overpowering a jailer on May 12, 1897, and escaping.

They were out again, and while they were out, the White Cap hierarchy tasked them with committing the triple assassinations of White Cap Prosecutor J. R. Penland, Dr. Z. D. Massey, and of course Deputy Sheriff Tom Davis.

GREEN AND HENDRICKS.

Paid to Kill Four Sevier County Citizens.

Sevierville, Tenn., July 21.—The report to the effect that a massacre of Tom Davis, J. R. Penland and two other parties had been arranged has proved all too true, but as yet the plans have been frustrated.

The Journal representative called on Messrs. Penland and Davis this afternoon and asked them about the report and they stated that the report was true. Mr. Davis stated that it was quite fortunate for himself and Penland that one of the other gentlemen, whose name he would not divulge, had been notified of the plans in time to be placed on their guard. He stated further that the plan had been laid last Saturday and would have been carried into effect Tuesday night but for the fact that one of the gentlemen to be put out of the way had a whitecap friend who came to him and warned him of the affair.

Knowing the plans of the whitecaps to have the deed committed, Deputy Davis went to General Mynatt and Judge Nelson and after a consultation it was decided that Davis should organize a posse and if possible capture the entire crowd that was to gather at the council of war. Accordingly, Mr. Davis summoned a posse of deputies and late last night set out for the place of meeting, fifteen miles above this city. The whitecaps, however, heard of the movement and they changed their place for meeting. Davis and his crowd rode all night, but were unable to locate the parties and returned to town early this morning.

The plan agreed upon was that Green and Hendricks, two men who have been sentenced to the penitentiary for twenty years each and who broke jail a few months ago, were to commit the deed. Money enough had been made up by the whitecaps to pay their expense of getting out of the country. Further, all whitecaps who were known to be enemies of Davis and who would be suspicious of the deed, were to be in the presence of some of Davis' friends, so that an alibi could be established.

The fact that the plan has been nipped in the bud will no doubt put an end to it, at least for the present and an effort will be made to capture Green and Hendricks and place them in jail again.

All precautions are being taken to prevent the murderous gang from getting in their work and it is hoped that there will be no outbreak.—Knoxville Journal.

The Robbery of John Burnett[73]
November 7, 1896[74]

The next documented crime in the endgame crime spree was the robbery of an old pensioner named John Burnett, who owned a small hillside farm six miles west of Sevierville, in the foothills of Chilhowee Mountain. Burnett earned very little income from his little farm, but it was well known he received a pension of twenty-four dollars a month, a right handsome sum. And the Burnett robbery is another example of using newspaper articles to more accurately date-stamp an event.

With winter drawing near, it was time for Burnett to purchase the necessities his family would need while they waited for spring—shoes, hats, cloaks—and for the older boys, new suits. Burnett went to the bank and cashed his pension check, and evidently withdrew the funds from two other deposited checks, because when he returned home he had seventy-two dollars.

It makes one wonder whether or not it was his modus operandi, but Pleas Wynn sat outside the bank that day whittling, and apparently watched as the bank teller handed Burnett that large sum of money. Robbing an aged pensioner like Burnett would have likely looked like easy pickings, and an opportunity hard to pass up for a crook like Wynn.

That evening, while drinking and playing cards upstairs at Yett & Trotter's Store, Pleas allegedly shared this information with George Thurmer, and Sam and Joe Jenkins. The Jenkins brothers operated a livery stable and a "blind tiger," a place that sold illegal whiskey.

When the strong liquor had taken effect, Pleas shared what he had seen and suggested they rob Burnett. It would be as simple as frightening the old man, stealing his money, then disappearing into the night. Even

---

[73] Crozier, 171
[74] THE WHITE CAP LAW HOLDS GOOD, *The Journal and Tribune*, Knoxville, Tennessee, October 20, 1897

though Thurmer was what might be considered a "career criminal" today, he was initially reluctant, as he had recently been pardoned out of the penitentiary for the 1890 murder of Knoxville police officer George Hoyle.

The conversation that took place convincing Thurmer to participate in the armed robbery is probably representative of many similar conversations, where Whitecap methods were used by Sevier County's criminal element as nothing less than a means to a nefarious end.[75]

> "This was a new field of business to Thurmer, and at first he protested against it, saying:
>
> "I have just returned from serving a term in the penitentiary, and we will all get caught up with, and then I will have another job an [*sic*] my hands."
>
> "You are the very man we need, George," argued Wynn. "You must go; we can't do it without you."
>
> "Pshaw, George. They ain't one bit o' danger. They can't do nothin' with a White-cap," chimed in Joe Jenkins.

The men drank into the evening, then eventually mounted horses and rode to the Burnett homeplace. They crashed into the Burnett home, armed, threatened Burnett then struck him with the butt of a pistol and demanded the money. His eldest daughter, having seen her father bloodied, knew where the money was hidden and pulled open a drawer and handed it to Pleas.

As there is no honor among thieves, it was reported in the Crozier book that Pleas claimed to have only been handed thirty-nine dollars, that he divided equally, then kept the balance for himself.

---

[75] Crozier, 171-172

About a week after the Burnett robbery, on November 15, 1896,[76] Bob Catlett and Bob Wade were indicted for rocking and shooting the home of Walter Maples. Their actions that night precipitated the final nail in the coffin of Sevier County Whitecapping.

The Robbery of Andrew Henderson
December 1896

The home invasion robbery of one of the best-loved men in the county, the venerable Andrew Henderson, known to almost everyone as Old Uncle Andy, was reported in the December 16, 1896, Knoxville Tribune as having occurred "last Sunday morning."[77] The article stated the robbers "were clothed in Mother Hubbard dresses and had black calico tied over their faces."

With his wife, Sarah, Andrew Henderson farmed a fertile riverfront plot in the Henderson Springs area and was known as a plain-speaker, a man of opinions which he shared liberally.

His disdain for the White Caps was well-known.

Couple that with the common belief that Henderson kept a right smart sum of money in his home, this gave the White Caps two reasons to target the old man.

Born January 13, 1818, Old Uncle Andy had saved his money for all of his 78 years, and had accumulated more than $2,000, which he kept in a safe in his home in the form of gold. Late on a chilly late-November evening, the marauders came calling.

Someone in the band had knowledge of the old man's habits and knew that he kept his loaded shotgun near his bed at all times. Uncle Andy's slumber was shattered when the muzzle of a White cap's shotgun crashed

---

[76] Dated by the Indictment of Bob Catlett and Bob Wade
[77] MOTHER HUBBARDS, *The Knoxville Tribune*, Knoxville, Tennessee, December 16, 1896

through his bedroom window, along with the command, "Hold up your hands."[78] The old couple froze in the bed as others of the White Cap band broke down the door.

Uncle Andy was dragged from his bed and shoved around the room a little before being forced to the safe and ordered to open it. Fear and a possibly fading memory made it difficult to remember the combination, but ultimately he did and the safe door opened, revealing the shiny gold. The robbers seized it .

Old Uncle Andy also usually kept some smooth liquor on hand for his customary morning dram. The bandits knew that, too, and quickly found a two-gallon demijohn of whiskey with the seal still unbroken. With the money and moonshine in hand, the White Caps put a pistol in the old man's face and warned him, "Old man, if you ever cheep this, your life instead of your gold will pay the penalty."

Their mission was complete, they celebrated their success with gulps of whiskey, whooping and hollering as they rode away from the Henderson home

"White Caps, White Caps!" they shouted, "Hurrah for the White Caps! Clear the way—the White Caps are coming!"

They passed farm after farm, still cheering their victory with alcohol-fueled hoots and laughter until they drew near the Sevierville outskirts. There they slowed, quieted and dispersed.

Andrew and Sarah Henderson remained in their bed until ten o'clock the next morning, afraid the White Caps were still lurking. Later in the day, Old Uncle Andy sent for his nephew, William Henderson. When he arrived the old man burst into tears, crying, "Bill, I am ruined! They robbed me of all my gold and left me without a cent.!"

A reward was posted in connection with the robbery, but there is no evidence the bandits were ever brought to justice. From that November

---

[78] Crozier, 177

night through the next couple of months, Old Uncle Andy's mental state deteriorated rapidly, the loss of his life savings seemingly costing him his lucidity. He died broke and broken on February 23, 1897. He was buried in Shiloh Memorial Cemetery. Sarah "Sallie" Pickle Henderson died July 11, 1916, and was buried next to her husband.

The crime that would doom the White Caps came about two weeks after Andrew Henderson's robbery.

15

The Murder for Hire of Bill and Laura Whaley

Bill and Laura Whaley were a young couple whose love for each other far exceeded their material possessions and, frankly, their prospects for an abundant future in Sevier County. Both were the product of hardscrabble upbringings, households where the focus was on scratching a tomorrow out of today. Laura McMahan Whaley was the daughter of Blackburn "B. B." McMahan and his wife, Susan Henry McMahan. Theirs was a working-class household west of Sevierville, one of modest means but sound principles. William H. "Bill" Whaley's childhood was even more basic. He was the son of William Thomas Larrimore and Caroline Whaley, who were wed in 1872 in Hamblen County. Census records for 1880 show Larrimore as a resident of the Hamblen County Jail. Perhaps that is why Caroline chose her maiden name for her two daughters and Bill, who was born in 1877.

Laura Whaley was a year older than her husband, and they were married in December 1892, when they were both still kids.

In December 1895, William Whaley leased a plot of land and a small house from Bob Catlett. It was just a small place where Bill expected to raise a little corn to supplement his income as an employee on Bob

107

Catlett's farm. The Whaleys entered into a sharecropping agreement, in which they were to pay their rent in the form of a portion of Bill's corn crop.

At the time of the lease agreement, the house on the road between Sevierville and Knoxville was occupied by the family of Walter Maples. But when the Whaleys showed up to move in, Maples refused to vacate. Catlett made provision for the Whaleys to take up temporary residence in another cabin he owned until Maples could be evicted.

Bob Catlett was the eldest son of James Catlett, who owned 600 of the best riverfront acres in Sevier County. The younger Catlett had a reputation for unpredictability. There was a wild and reckless streak in him that got broader and deeper when he drank. He had acquired a taste for strong drink while in his youth, and when he got drunk, his merely overbearing personality became intensely obnoxious, even dangerous. He was known to have crossed the line into downright meanness and cruelty on occasion, even to the point of causing the deaths of others.[79]

Catlett's father facilitated his son's skill at buying and selling superior horse flesh while failing to insist that Bob get an education. It would prove crucial to Bob's future.

Bob Catlett married the former Mary Ann Wade, daughter of another prominent Sevier Countian, J. J. Wade. By the mid-1890s he was the father of nine, had reduced his alcohol intake, but when he did drink he became even more volatile—he was still mean and angry. He had not been an early member of the White Caps, so by the time he was initiated, the White Caps' focus was less on raising the county's morals and more on personal vendettas and settling old scores.

According to the True Bill returned against Catlett and his brother-in-law Bob Wade, the two of them went to the house where the Whaleys were staying with a demand. Catlett wanted Laura Whaley to do what he

---

[79] Crozier, 161-162

could not—write a Whitecap note ordering Walter Maples to get out of that house or face a White Cap whipping.

Laura at first refused. But after a warning from Wade that Catlett was drunk and would kill her if she didn't comply, she consented to the demand—she had no choice, as Bob Wade also held her husband at gunpoint.

She copied a notice which Catlett gave her:

> "Walter Maples:
>
> If you do not move out of this house in five days, the penalty of the White Caps will be visited on you. The time is half up now.—White Caps."

In an attempt to make the letter appear to be an authentic Whitecap letter, Catlett cursed the 19-year-old woman, "Damn you, don't dot your i's and cross your t's." He then *administered the White Cap oath to her*, which guaranteed vengeance on her if she revealed what had happened or any secrets of the White Caps. He demanded she surrender one of her dress skirts, which he cut into a White Cap disguise.

Catlett and Wade then left for Maples' house, taking Bill Whaley along at gunpoint. They forced Whaley to nail the note to the door of Maples' home before pelting the house with rocks—and even a blast from a shotgun—to make sure Maples did not overlook the warning. Maples and his wife and family shuddered, terrified in the bed during the incident, some of the shot going into their bed.

Within days, the Maples family fled and the Whaleys moved in.

Laura was also capable of keeping records, and she was meticulous when it came to her household finances and her husband's employment records. She knew, as did Bill, that Catlett had not paid him for the work he had done on Catlett's farm.

In the early spring of 1896, Bill Whaley had bought some hogs from Catlett on a bill of sale recorded at the Sevier County Courthouse, with payment to come later. Whaley raised his corn crop at his new home over the summer months. In September, Laura Whaley, now approaching the delivery date for the couple's first child, calculated that her husband had worked enough unpaid days on the Catlett farm to have satisfied the debt for the hogs. With that knowledge, Bill sold the hogs to pay off other obligations

Late September splashed the East Tennessee hills with a patchwork of warm color that covered the spectrum from sunflower yellow to mousy brown. But the season brought little comfort or delight to the young Whaleys, even as they anticipated the birth of their first baby. Laura Whaley's older sister, Elizabeth "Lizzie" McMahan Chandler, had come to stay with Laura and help her through the childbirth. Lizzie had recently abandoned her own husband, John, having concluded he was worthless— he was also a White Cap.

When Bob Catlett learned that Bill Whaley had sold the hogs, the volatile side of his nature took control, and he rushed to the Whaley home in a rage. On arrival he found Bill Whaley gathering his corn, cursed him for having sold the mortgaged hogs, then ordered him to "let the corn alone." Catlett threatened to have Whaley arrested over the hog sale. Whaley attempted to explain that the bill for the hogs was covered by the unpaid days he had worked at Catlett's farm, but Catlett refused to agree and secured a warrant for Whaley's arrest.

The stress of it all was too much for Laura, who knew that in the hour when she would need him most, he might be arrested for having heeded her counsel over the hogs and the unpaid wages. She went into premature labor.

Mollie Lillard Whaley was born too soon—Sept. 23, 1896—to a mother too young and too fretful about her future.

Rou Catlett, Bob's daughter, was a schoolteacher who possessed all the kindness and compassion that was lacking in her father. She visited Laura shortly after her new baby was born to congratulate the parents and see the infant Mollie. Rou and Laura were of the same age and temperament, and perhaps that is why Laura felt enough kinship to her to open up about the night Rou's father and Bob Wade forced her to write the Maples note, as well about the hog deal and the threat to have Bill Whaley arrested.

Rou could apparently touch a soft spot in her father that no one else could, and she confronted him about his disagreement with the Whaleys. She persuaded him to cancel both the debt for the pigs and the arrest warrant for Bill. Later, Bob Catlett went back to the Whaley home and told them the debt was paid and that the warrant would be canceled.

But he also knew that Laura had betrayed the White Caps' secret oath and told her, "For this, you shall die." Catlett ordered the Whaleys off his land by the next day.

Believing their landlord perfectly capable of carrying out his threat, Bill Whaley bundled up his wife, still weak from childbirth, and his six-day-old daughter and loaded them onto a bed in the back of a wagon and relocated them, along with his sister-in-law, Lizzie. They moved into a hillside cabin about a half-mile behind the farmhouse of Elkanah Mitchell Wynn, the former High Sheriff of Sevier County.

Bill Whaley never got his corn, and the debt for the hogs was never canceled. Based on the theory that a secret known by two people is not really a secret, it was virtually inevitable that Laura Whaley's account of the White Cap note would begin to weave its way around the community, particularly after she also told her own mother about it. And the story would travel even faster since it involved a member of one of Sevier County's more prominent families.

It didn't take long for the story to find its way into the ear of Tom Davis. To him it sounded like the wall of White Cap secrecy beginning to

111

crack, and he seized the opportunity to bring the case directly before a grand jury—normally a charge as minor as the one Catlett and Wade were accused of would be stifled by a Justice of the Peace. Davis subpoenaed the Whaleys to testify in November 1896.

Bill and Laura, along with Lizzie and the infant Molly, all came to court. Laura told the entire story under oath from the witness stand, perhaps the single most courageous act of anyone not named Tom Davis in the White Cap saga.

A True Bill was handed down against Bob Catlett and Bob Wade for the rock-and-buckshot assault on the Maples house, a relatively minor charge, but significant, nonetheless.

Indictment.

"State of Tennessee.

Sevier County.

Circuit Court, November Term 1896. The Grand Jurors for the State of Tennessee upon their oaths present, that Robert Catlett and Robert Wade, on the 15th day of November 1896, in the State and County aforesaid, unlawfully and wilfully did assault, strike and beat one W.H.Maples, by shooting into his house, the said W.H.Maples and family being in said house at the time, in the peace of our State, then and being contrary to the Statutes against the peace and dignity of the State.

G.Mc.Henderson, Attorney General.

Endorsed.

A true Bill.

T.C.Fox, Foreman of the Grand Jury.

No.8.

The State.

vs.

Robert Catlett et al.

Assault.

Walter Maples, Pros.

Filed Nov. 1896.   R.C.Fowler, Clerk.

The indictment, or True Bill, of Robert "Bob" Catlett and Robert "Bob" Wade for the Rocking and Shooting of Walter Maples' home. Laura McMahan Whaley testified against Catlett and Wade, and it was for this reason that Bob Catlett wanted the Whaleys "put out of the way."

Lizzie Chandler and Mollie were waiting in office following the court action, when Laura Whaley walked in.

"Lizzie, as I came through the hall I met Bob Catlett and Bob Wade. *They* will kill us."

White Caps typically dragged poor, defenseless women from their homes, and either two of them held her while another or others lashed her back, or she was forced to embrace a tree, and held while the withes were administered.

Probably an accurate sketch of the cowards masking their faces, while armed and on horseback.

Sketches by artist H. P. Ijams illustrate some of the terrorizing activities of the White-Caps. Knoxville News Sentinel June 2, 1929

Millard Fillmore Maples and wife Laura
High Sheriff, Sevier County Tennessee, 1894-1898

Thomas Houston Davis served as a Deputy Sheriff and the High Sheriff of Sevier County during the White Caps saga, and is generally considered the driving force behind the eradication of Whitecapping in Sevier County. He was the Police Chief in Jellico from 1911-1912, then ran for sheriff in Knox County, losing by 164 votes in 1920. He then served as Police Chief in Etowah from 1920-1922.

Laura McMahan Whaley
Courtesy of the Peter H. Prince Collection
University of Tennessee

Elizabeth "Lizzie" McMahan Chandler
Courtesy of the Peter H. Prince Collection
University of Tennessee

John S. Springs, Postmaster, Emert's Cove
Hangman who placed hoods and nooses on
Catlett Tipton and Pleas Wynn, 5 July 1899
"Any man or set of men who would go at the dead hours of
midnight, under the cover of darkness with masks on their faces,
and drag a poor defenseless woman from her home and lash her
back is a base coward and not worthy of citizenship."

Sketch of the Whaley Cabin on the property
of Captain E. M. Wynn

Bill and Laura Whaley were shot to death here on
28 December 1896

James Catlett Tipton, Convicted murderer of William "Bill" Whaley

Pleasant (Pleas or Shorty) D. Wynn
Convicted murderer of Laura McMahan Whaley and
William "Bill" Whaley

Sevier County Circuit Court cases were moved from the Second Judicial Circuit Court under Judge Hicks, and placed under the jurisdiction of Judge Thomas Amos Rogers Nelson, Jr. (pictured above). This legal action was instrumental in the eradication of Whitecapping in Sevier County, and was frowned upon by many Sevier Countians who believed their neighboring county, Knox County, was meddling.

James Royal "J. R." Penland
Prosecutor of Sevier County White Caps

122

Dr. Zachary David "Z. D." Massey was instrumental in the eradication of Whitecapping in Sevier County. Dr. Massey had an informant, from whom he passed information to Deputy Sheriff Tom Davis while he was pursuing Green and Hendricks in Texas. Dr. Massey was also targeted for assassination by the White Caps.

-Photo courtesy of Carroll McMahan, Sevier County Historian.

Advertisement from the Sevierville Star, March 1, 1895. James Catlett Tipton allegedly secured money given to him by William R. "Bob" Catlett to kill the Whaleys in a safe in this store.

Advertisement from the Sevierville Star, February 22, 1895. Lizzie McMahan Chandler identified Pleas Wynn from an upstairs room in this hotel on January 4, 1897.

16

"Put Out of the Way"

B ob Catlett was not the first man to develop such an acute sense of self-importance that he came to believe the rules were for everyone but him. The high and mighty often fall into the same false confidence, and others typically suffer as a result. Undoubtedly because he was a prominent landowner and White Cap, he felt some measure of legal invincibility in Sevier County. Or maybe because he was simply filled with hate, and along with that sense of entitlement, he just could not let it go.

He and Bob Wade had resorted to using White Cap methods as a means to a different end—they were wealthy landowners and Walter Maples was a tenant—so just like Cummings pointed out in his thesis, "... unsatisfied with a slow and ineffective court system, the landowners saw in the whitecaps an opportunity to expedite their potential legal problems with troublesome tenants."[80]

---

[80] Cummings, 20

Why would Bob Catlett (a *have*) promise the Whaleys (*have nots*) a cabin he owned, knowing full well another tenant was already living there? Because he could.

The rocking and pelting of Walter Maples' home with a little buckshot should never have even made it to the grand jury—this was clearly the type of criminal activity justices of the peace routinely dismissed. And as far as property damage, Catlett owned the cabin. Even still, a guilty plea to a charge he likely could have gotten reduced, and maybe a small fine he certainly could have afforded, and the whole thing would have been over with. But he could not let go. He and Wade were arrested on the Maples charges, made their bond, and were released.

He was a man of influence and an entitled bully with a mean streak. He did not like being crossed, especially by a couple of kids whose entire net worth was probably less than the bond he posted to get out of jail.

Bob Catlett seethed.

Sevier County was no longer a safe place for the Whaleys, so they set their sights on relocating to the Coal Creek community in nearby Anderson County—Laura is said to have had family there. Bill went first, to find work and save money for the move. It took him about a month, but he accomplished his goals, and sometime in December he came back for his family. Immediately upon his return, though, he was brought low with a severe case of the grippe, as influenza was called then. Upper respiratory infection was a serious killer at the time, often claiming small children when a common cold advanced to untreatable pneumonia.

Bill Whaley was bedridden with fever, a cough, and body aches, and all he could do was wait it out—it delayed his plan to move out of Sevier County, and away from Bob Catlett. Catlett's anger had not subsided since the November grand jury session—it was lying there deep in his gut, smoldering deep inside the ashes of a fire that everyone thought was out.

Bob Catlett's social status and membership in the White Caps organization, which had digressed very quickly from vigilantes upholding

Victorian morals, to not much more than roaming bands of thugs and robbers settling old scores and keeping tenant farmers and sharecroppers in line. If Catlett wanted a job done he could find somebody willing to do it. So, he began asking around if this person or that had any interest in a couple of homicides for hire.

His initial offer was $50—fifty dollars offered by one of the "Haves" to kill a couple of "Have-nots."

He did not get any immediate takers, but he kept asking, and he kept upping the price on the Whaleys heads. Finally he asked James Catlett Tipton, a 35-year old carpenter and blacksmith who had been named for Bob Catlett's father. By then the offer had doubled—$100 to kill the Whaleys.

"J. C.," as Tipton was known in his native Sevier County, had a mid-level education, was well-liked and thought of as bright and handsome, with a little touch of wildness in his nature. He was a fisherman, and a hunter with a reputation as a dead-on marksman with a pistol or a rifle. Tipton was born August 18, 1861, and by age 23 he was working as carpenter, helping build a new resort hotel known as Seaton's Summer City 8 miles north of Sevierville. It was there he met Mary Seaton, the daughter of the owner of Seaton's Springs, and proprietor of the hotel Tipton was helping construct.

Much to the disappointment of the Seatons, their pretty daughter and the carpenter fell in love, and despite their disapproval Mary Seaton and J. C. Tipton wed.

A hundred bucks was a lot of money, in that time and place, enough to get a man through the impending winter and see him through to spring. Bob Catlett met J. C. Tipton at Fred Emert's store one day and asked to speak with him in a back room, along with Bob Wade. Catlett talked about his vendetta against the Whaleys and that he wanted them "put out of the way" for their testimony, which had gotten him and Wade indicted. Catlett told Tipton he wanted to make an example of the Whaleys, "to make an example of them to teach people that they could not swear against him."[81] But Tipton, not bereft of intelligence, declined the offer as had others before him.

That very night, a group of men including Tipton, Catlett and Wade, William Wynn and Jesse Atchley,[82] went to a meeting at the Odd Fellows Lodge in Pigeon Forge, and as they were riding back to Sevierville they stopped by a turnip patch near Henderson's Island. Tipton, who had been riding in a buggy with other men, distributed some turnips to them. But when the trip resumed, Catlett prevailed on Wade to ride the buggy and let Tipton ride Wade's horse so they could talk. Catlett again broached the subject of the paid killings, and again Tipton refused. Catlett then handed Tipton an envelope containing four $20 bills and one $20 gold piece. He told Tipton the money would be his when the Whaleys were eliminated. Tipton took the envelope home, but the next day he asked J. R. Yett to place the money in the safe at Yett's store. Two days later Tipton retrieved the envelope and gave it back to Catlett, once again declining to kill the Whaleys. Catlett told Tipton he was glad he turned the offer down, because he thought he could get it done for half the mount he had offered him.

In all, Catlett tried more than a dozen times to enlist Tipton. One can only speculate as to why Tipton finally acquiesced, but it is not a stretch to imagine that Catlett berated Tipton, perhaps even questioning whether or not the White Caps oath meant anything at all, or was just empty words.

Eventually, Tipton agreed to murder the Whaleys—for $50—with Catlett agreeing to pay the bond or legal fees that might be incurred. Tipton told Catlett he had had discussions with a friend, Pleas Wynn, and Wynn had agreed to accompany Tipton.

Pleasant D. "Pleas" Wynn was also known as "Shorty," for his diminutive stature. "Pleasant" was a name that may have been misplaced

---

[81] Crozier, 208
[82] Ibid

on Wynn, who was born in Pigeon Forge in 1869 and lived in adulthood in Sevierville. He possessed the innate shrewdness of a Sevier County native, and he had not done well in school. He was active, strong, fast and competitive, and he never backed down from a fight.

As an adult, married to the former Mary Thomas, Pleas Wynn failed to settle into the role of upstanding citizen and head of a household; he was a little too fond of alcohol and games of chance. He never had what could be described as a profession, though he had at one time served as a jailer when his father was High Sheriff of Sevier County from 1886 to 1890. The elder Wynn was the owner of the home into which Bill and Laura Whaley had moved after Bob Catlett evicted them.

Both Pleas Wynn and J. C. Tipton knew Bill Whaley. Wynn knew him "tolerably well." "I was barely acquainted with William Whaley," Tipton said, "I knew him when I saw him." That was about how well Wynn knew Laura Whaley, but Tipton had never seen her before.

Perhaps that lack of a personal connection made their assignment a little easier. It couldn't have been the blood money, fifty bucks to be split two ways. In any event, the conspirators did their best to plot their crime, with established alibis, precise timing, White Cap masks and the cover of darkness.

Bob Catlett arranged for his brother Jim to hold the $50, and deliver it to Tipton when the executions were carried out. On December 28, 1896, Bob Catlett harnessed up four horses to take to North Carolina, ostensibly to do some trading. He needed to be somewhere other than Sevier County that evening.

Pleas Wynn met Catlett at M. R. Rawling's saddle shop that morning, and helped him fix the girth on a saddle.[83] Later on that day, Catlett and Wynn were at Loveday's stable, where Catlett ushered Wynn into a back room and first mentioned "putting the Whaleys out of the way."[84] Catlett

---

[83] Crozier, 205
[84] Ibid

asked Wynn if he and Tipton had come to an agreement, and Wynn said they had. Catlett told him he wanted it done that night.

Catlett left Sevierville about noon with the four horses, believing he had established a sufficient alibi. He stopped for the night sixteen miles from Sevierville, at the Jones Cove home of George Roland, with whom Catlett sat up late talking.

Wynn and Tipton made it widely known they were going fishing on that cold and moonless night in Hardin's Pool, less than a mile south of Sevierville, on the west fork of the Little Pigeon River.

In their confessions, both Wynn and Tipton disputed the truthfulness of the contents of the following paragraphs, vowing that the statements constituted perjury. Considering the White Caps were a brood of vipers and den of thieves, either version is believable, though neither Tipton nor Wynn had anything to gain by disputing the claims made against Wynn. Allegedly, at about 5:00 PM, Wynn dropped by the blind tiger operated by Joe Jenkins on the edge of Sevierville on the east fork of the Little Pigeon.

> "I was at home on the night of the killing. Wynn in brother Joe's room, a little after dark. They were talking low. Deft. got a pint or a bottle of whiskey and came to my room door, and picked up a number 38 pistol from the fire board and said, 'I want this tonight' and stuck it in his pocket."[85]

Wynn exited out the back door and worked his way to a ford about a mile down the riverbank, where he met Tipton at the home of Ben Bailey, Tipton's brother-in-law. Tipton retrieved a shotgun from a tool chest.

Tipton and Wynn crossed the river in a boat belonging to Mark McCowan, and followed a footpath to the Whaley home. Darkness was

---

[85] Jep Jenkins testimony, Transcript from PLEAS WYNN V. STATE, TRIAL I, Monday, November 15, through Friday November 26, 1897

no impediment; Wynn knew the path well because it was on his father's farm, and he and his wife had lived in the same cabin shortly after they married in May 1889.

Wynn and Tipton approached the small cabin quietly, then hid in a stable within twenty yards of the house. Inside the cabin, Bill and Laura Whaley and their infant daughter Molly Lillard Whaley had visitors—Bill's brother John and Laura's sister Lizzie McMahan Chandler. While huddling in the dark, wintry silence, listening to the conversation inside the cabin, Wynn coughed.

John Whaley had opened the door to leave when Wynn coughed, and he heard the cough. "He went to the door opened it and then shut it and said he heard some one cough, and took up the gun and a light and went out and nailed a piece across the crib door. He came in, left the rifle and started for home. There was a bright light in the fire. Was using oak and pine."[86]

It was about 7:00 PM.

---

[86] Lizzie Chandler testimony, Transcript from PLEAS WYNN V. STATE, TRIAL I

17

In Cold Blood

December days are even shorter in the hills and hollers of east Tennessee, and temperatures that are chilly turn downright frigid when night falls.

There was not much in the Whaley cabin to keep the cold out except a fireplace, nightclothes and bedcovers. So, with the fire burning brightly in the hearth, Laura Whaley laid her Mollie—then 96 days old—in the arms of the baby's feverish father and joined him under the warming blankets. Lizzie Chandler was in another bed in an opposite corner of the room.

"I went and closed the door and then went to bed. I had been there about five minutes when I heard a noise at the door. There are two doors, one back and one front. The noise was at the front door, and it came open. Two men came in. Billy jumped up and said. 'Have you come to kill us? We are willing to suffer anything, but don't kill us.' Laura said, 'Lord, Lord, Lord, Lord. If you will spare our lives, just do anything else you want with us. If you will kill us, let me give my little babe to my sister' and she brought it and put the baby's head on my left arm, then the gun fired, and a body fell, sounded like Billy's from the position he was in, then another shot and a body fell, sounded like Laura's.[87]

There had been no ceremony about the assassins' deed; no words of contempt or vengeance, no blows struck as a tortuous prelude. In a matter of seconds it was over. A man squeezes his trigger finger twice and a baby is orphaned. And without ever saying a word and still masked, Tipton and Wynn left—Wynn never removed the "number 38 pistol" from his pocket. They probably felt confident their identities had not been compromised, as they were two of 650-1500 potential suspects … but Lizzie Chandler caught a glimpse of one of their profiles:

"The low heavy set man had something over his face. I got a good look at him on side of face. He rather leaned forward and mask flew out. The medium sized man had no mask. The low heavy set man had a gun as he came in the door. He was in front. Neither man spoke a word."[88]

Lizzie Chandler's testimony is somewhat confusing, in that she described the two killers as "the low heavy set man" and the "medium sized man," and even though she said the "medium sized man had no mask on" it was Pleas Wynn she pointed to when asked if she could recognize the killer.

John Whaley was back at the home he shared with his and Bill's mother when he heard the shots that killed his brother and sister-in-law.

"I had not been gone ten minutes when I heard the shot. Had just sat down to supper. Mother said to me, 'Will had shot

---

[87] Lizzie Chandler testimony, Transcript from PLEAS WYNN V. STATE, TRIAL I
[88] Ibid

somebody.' I got up and went up there. Walked some and run part of the way. I hollowed outside of the house and asked what was the matter. Lizzie said, come in and see. When I went in I found them both dead on the floor. I then went right back to mother's and told her about it. I staid in the house about two minutes and then went old man Vests."[89]

After recrossing the river, Wynn and Tipton quickly retreated to Sevierville, where they split up and set Part B of their plan into action. Tipton returned his shotgun to the tool chest at Ben Bailey's. Wynn went to O. L. Montgomery's and asked Montgomery to go fishing. Montgomery was sick and declined Wynn's offer. Wynn asked the time, and Montgomery told him it was nearly nine o'clock.[90]

Tipton and Wynn met again at the courthouse square and returned to the home of Mark McCowan, from whom they had borrowed the boat. They asked McCowan if he wanted to go fishing with them, but he told them he had sick family at his house and declined. It did not really matter; they had made sure someone had seen them around that time some distance from the Whaley home.

In truth, they did go fishing, in a manner that not only guaranteed they would catch some fish, but would attract some attention to their activity. Wynn and Tipton took McCowan's boat again and pushed out into the river again, lit two sticks of dynamite, and tossed them into the water. Their tally: five suckers (carp) and a salmon (trout).

Wynn and Tipton returned the boat to McCowan and then buried their masks on the riverbank. Tipton took the salmon and Wynn the suckers, and they returned to Sevierville as the clock in the courthouse struck 10 that Monday night. And then they went home.

[89] John Whaley testimony, Transcript from PLEAS WYNN V. STATE, TRIAL I
[90] Crozier, 204

Though no one was appointed to count, it was said that 500 people visited the scene of the Whaley killings. Many saw the disfigured bodies and reflected on the orphaned baby girl, and were repulsed by the unbounded wickedness of the act—the cruelty and the wantonness.

Two doctors, Dr. E. H. Pierce and Dr. Z. D. Massey, testified in the first trial and described the injuries to the Whaleys. As you might imagine the details were graphic, but they both mentioned something that made its way into some narratives—"on one hand, the little finger was missing, and the hand somewhat mutilated".[91] This led some to speculate that the killers had removed the finger as proof that their deed had been done. Dr. Massey believed the missing finger was a defensive wound, that she had moved her hand over her face as the gun was fired.

Their killing was the tipping point in the White Caps Saga—Bill and Laura were just kids, just getting started with their lives and their infant daughter—Sevier County had finally had enough. Nothing about the Whaleys signaled they deserved this. Their murders went infinitely beyond the scope of the White Caps' initial focus, that of ridding Sevier County of some undesirables.

There was instant scorn and disdain for the unknown killers and an immediate call for them to be apprehended and to face the consequences of their deed. The countywide fear that criticizing the White Caps might bring on their hateful wrath seemed to evaporate almost within hours of the Whaley deaths in the cold December darkness. There were open calls for legal retribution, and a righteous avalanche of indignation rolled over the hills. Anti-White Cap sentiment grew by the hour and by the day until such talk became open and unending. Even members of the organization itself turned away in disgust. This was not what most of them had signed up for.

---

[91] Dr. E. H. Pierce testimony, Transcript from PLEAS WYNN V. STATE, TRIAL I

Suddenly, anyone known to have ties to the White Caps came under suspicion, and that was a considerable number. Who did it and why? And who knew who did it?

Bob Catlett's blood money had not included killing anyone other than the Whaleys, certainly not a baby. Pleas Wynn and J. C. Tipton knew their victims were not alone in the cabin, but they believed that since their faces were masked and they never spoke meant their identities were secure. And they were for close to a week. But whether his boastful nature got the best of him or alcohol got hold of his tongue, Wynn simply could not keep his actions to himself. Or was the testimony that implicated Wynn perjured, as both he and Tipton claimed?

At some point shortly after the murders, Wynn was allegedly playing cards with Sam Jenkins and asked him if Jenkins's brother, Joe, had told him that Wynn had been at the blind tiger the night of the killings.

"Yes," Jenkins said, "he told me all about it."

"Well for God's sake, don't say a word about it," Wynn exclaimed. "By Goddamn, I did kill the Whaleys, and it took a damned sight of nerve to do it. But I got one hundred dollars for the job."

Almost everything in Wynn's alleged statement to Jenkins stretched the truth. But he had indeed been part of the conspiracy, and his involvement made him a murderer, even if he did not fire his pistol and only collected $25 "for the job." By week's end, though, the word was getting out about Pleas Wynn's role in the murder plot.

On Friday, New Year's Day, Tom Davis returned to Sevier County from East Bernstadt, Kentucky, where he had taken a fugitive named J. J. Robison into custody. Arising early Saturday, Davis rode to Catlettsburg, where an agitated crowd was still discussing the Whaley murders, which had happened five days prior. Davis gathered what information he could and rode straightway to the murder scene with a promise that he would see justice served in the case.

At the cabin Davis found Lizzie Chandler, still weeping over the loss of her sister and brother-in-law. She recounted the scene of horror to the deputy, along with the information that she had seen the face of one of the killers in profile that night.

"If I ever lay my eyes on that little, short man that did the shooting, I will know him," she told Davis. In truth, the man whose face she saw— Pleas Wynn—did not fire the fatal shots. This is a fact she could not have known, because she and the baby Mollie were covered by blankets when Tipton pulled the trigger on his shotgun. Davis, fearing for Lizzie Chandler's safety, ferried her away to his own home for protection.

Before sunup on Monday, January 4, 1897, a week to the day after the murders, Davis brought Lizzie Chandler to Sevierville. Davis seated her at an upstairs window in the Mitchell Hotel, overlooking the city center, to see if she might spot the man she had seen in the firelight the night of the killings. Hours passed. Then at about 11:00 a.m. the bereaved sister of Laura Whaley recoiled in horror and pointed to a man she saw saunter by the square.

"There goes the very man that killed sister and Bill Whaley."[92]

---

[92] Crozier, 73

18

The Killers Arrested and Jailed,
Not Without Incidents

Pleas Wynn was meandering among the crowd on the street below, "suspected by everybody" in the murders of Bill and Laura Whaley the week before.[93] Deputy Sheriff Tom Davis had been indefatigable in his mission to end Sevier County Whitecapping, and it must have been with great satisfaction that he walked downstairs inside the Mitchell Hotel and onto the street, where he arrested Wynn.

Lizzie Chandler had only recently come to Sevier County and may not have known Wynn by name, but she recognized him by his firelit-profile the night of the killings. And possibly by the distinctive long, blue coat he wore.

During the week since the murders, Lizzie had certainly told her horror tale to anyone who would listen. And who wouldn't? In addition, discretion never having been one of Pleas Wynn's stronger attributes, he had allegedly been bragging about his exploits, not just to Sam Jenkins, but to an acquaintance in Knoxville to whom he allegedly remarked:

---

[93] Crozier, 73

"I know deft Wynn when I see him. I saw him in Knoxville soon after the killing near Joe Clifts bar on the corner of Main and Crozier street. It was just about dark and I met deft Wynn there on the corner. I knew that he lived in Sevierville, and I asked him about the murder. I had all my talk with him right there on that corner. I asked deft. Wynn if Bob Catlett and Bob Wade were guilty and he said 'No by God, they've got the wrong sow by the ear.' Afterwards he said, 'I have blowed in two hundred dollars damned easy.' I asked him how, and he said 'I got it at two shots.'"[94]

It was only a few seconds after Lizzie Chandler's windowsill identification that Davis had the right sow by the ear. J. C. Tipton was also arrested within minutes of Wynn being taken into custody.

Wynn and Tipton were charged with first degree murder and brought before three justices of the peace that same day: Squires Pitner, Blalock and Pickens, and were discharged in a preliminary hearing.[95] The White Caps, through their perversion of the justice of the peace system, had seemingly won another questionable legal victory, "and sneered at the efforts being made by deputy sheriff Davis, but this did not effect Davis in the least. He only replied, 'He laughs best who laughs last.'"[96]

Wade was arrested the next day, Jan. 5, 1897, on charges of being an accessory before the fact in the Whaley murders. He claimed he had come to Sevierville to surrender, but his claim could not be proven or disproven.[97]

---

[94] Sam Finney testimony, Transcript from PLEAS WYNN V. STATE, TRIAL I
[95] TWO MEN PINCHED, *Knoxville Tribune*, Knoxville, Tennessee, January 6, 1897
[96] Crozier, 73-74
[97] TWO MEN PINCHED, January 6, 1897

Authorities had been alerted by telegram to arrest Bob Catlett in Asheville, N.C.—on his horse-trading excursion—on the same charge as Wade. Davis and Deputy J. E. Keener departed that day for North Carolina to retrieve their prisoner. When the deputies arrived, Catlett was his usual arrogant self, declaring, "I never got into any trouble yet I could not get out of," to which Davis responded, "Sometimes in a man's life the time comes when a man's money can't save him," and he pulled out a pair of handcuffs.

"You don't mean to put them on me, do you?" Catlett asked. "Yes sir," Davis said, "you will wear them back to Tennessee, or you or I one will die in North Carolina."

Neither one died, and in what must have been unbearable humiliation, Bob Catlett returned in handcuffs to the county in which he had been regarded an unstoppable force. He and Bob Wade were brought before Squire Wm. Atchley on Jan. 16, 1897, in connection with their roles in the murders. It was reported in the Knoxville Journal on January 20, 1897, that "the crowd began to gather at the court house and by ten o'clock more than a thousand people had packed into the court room."[98] Catlett was set free, but Wade was held for court on a $5,000 bond.

The arrests of all four of the principals in the Whaley murders, however, did not signal an end to the case, but they did stoke the embers of anger on both sides of the White Cap equation. For those outraged by the murders, they now had names and faces at which to direct their fury. White Cap members, however, were incensed that their wall of secrecy had been breached and that some of their compatriots—people whom they had sworn to protect—were now in the clutches of lawmen who had the capability to inflict real damage to the organization.

Meanwhile, Lizzie Chandler, by now divorced from the sluggard John Chandler, agreed for some reason to reunite with him and resume their

---

[98] WADE BOUND OVER, *The Knoxville Journal*, Knoxville, Tennessee, January 20, 1897

lives together in their old home. She climbed up behind him on his horse, ostensibly to go to a friend's house. But when her absence in Sevierville was noticed, Sheriff Maples and Deputy Davis took off in hot pursuit, overtaking them in the mountains just as they were about to cross over into North Carolina. John Chandler was arrested and jailed. Lizzie was spirited away to Knoxville for safety. Catlett had paid Chandler to try to get her out of the county so she could not testify.

Tension in Sevierville was palpable, with everyone wondering what would happen next. Would there be related killings? Would the defendants go into hiding or flee the county? Would a compromised court system somehow thwart the prosecution? Or would there be more arrests? It is likely that nearly everyone in town was a little more cautious about whom they were seen talking to in public.

For his part, Davis was aware that three of the four men implicated in the murders were free, and probably had both the capability and inclination to inflict revenge on him, his family, or others. It was said that many people estimated his life expectancy at less than a month, and certainly not long enough to present his case against the four to any grand jury.

The Sevier County Court had offered a $500 reward for information that led to the conviction of the Whaley murderers. W.P. Mitchell of Knoxville offered $100, and Sheriff Maples and Davis each offered $50.

During this period Davis received a White Cap threat that he would be assassinated unless he resigned his job as deputy. In response, the deputy gave the White Caps a poke in their hooded eye. He caught a train to Nashville, where he asked for and received an additional $500 reward from the state, authorized by Gov. Robert "Fiddlin' Bob" Taylor. On his trip home, Davis laid over in Knoxville for a few days. There he enlisted the assistance of Detectives C. A. Reeder and C. W. McCall, to find and interview potential witnesses in the Whaley case, who might have fled Sevier County in fear for their lives. That connection resulted in several trips between Sevierville and Knoxville for Davis, and that routine resulted in a near-miss on Davis's life.

At that time, small steam-powered paddle wheelers made regular trips between the markets in Knoxville and the docks at Catlettsburg, just north of Sevierville, hauling freight, goods and passengers. The French Broad River, which weaves through Sevier County from its source in North Carolina, eventually reaches a confluence with the Holsten River east of Knoxville. This is generally considered the head of the Tennessee River, which flows past downtown Knoxville. When the water was high enough, the shallow-water craft could even make it a little farther up the Little Pigeon River.

On one trip back from Knoxville, Davis was aboard the *Lucile Borden*, an 86-foot boat that could accommodate forty to fifty passengers on its 11-hour trip from Knoxville to Catlettsburg. Passenger fare was $1, and meals ranged from 15 to 25 cents. About halfway through its trip, a similar boat, the *Telephone*, came close enough that a burly black man named Chandler was able to step aboard the *Lucile Borden*. He began to ask questions about Davis and initiated a dispute with the boat's cook.

But Chandler kept glancing toward the bow of the boat looking for Davis. The deputy, suspicious of the man, circled around and approached the man from the stern. Encountering Davis, Chandler gave him a tremendous shove up against a railing, nearly knocking Davis into the river. Davis tried to draw his pistol with his right hand as he held the man at arm's length with his left.

Chandler also tried to draw his sidearm, described as a fine Smith & Wesson .44, but the hammer snagged on the lining of his pocket. Davis was able to get his gun out, and suddenly Chandler was staring helplessly and fearfully down its barrel, his face inches away from a hellish death.

Capt. James Edmund Newman, owner and skipper of the *Lucile Borden*, disarmed Chandler and helped Davis secure his prisoner. Davis brought his would-be assassin to Sevierville, and while they were in a court hearing, a second plot coalesced. This time the plan was to accost Davis at the Houk Bluff, about a mile and a half south of Sevierville, on the deputy's way home. Davis defeated that plot by simply remaining in town for the night.

AVERTED A KILLING

Capt. Newman Jumped in at the Right Moment.

Lively Time on the Steamboat Telephone with a Desperate Negro and His Ugly Pistol.

The steamer Telephone which left this city yesterday morning for up-river points, had a more eventful voyage than usual. A killing was averted only by the timely part taken in a scrimmage by Captain Newman, in charge of the steamer.

All went well on the trip until about 11:30 o'clock in the morning when the trouble occurred. A negro named Sam Chandler, who was a passenger on the boat for Sevierville, went to the cook of the boat, a negro named Sam Patterson and asked for a lunch. This was given him, but after he had devoured it he refused payment for it on the ground that he had already settled his bill. In the argument between the two negroes, Chandler applied the term liar to the cook, emphasizing his remarks with a wholesale use of oaths. When the cook started to get something to hit him with Chandler pulled a dangerous looking pistol, but before he could use it the cook had disappeared. Deputy Sheriff Davis of Sevier county happened to be on the boat. He was told of Chandler's pistol and a few minutes after order had been restored, started to arrest him. Chandler defied arrest and a scuffle ensued. Deputy Davis managed to draw his pistol and had it against the negro's breast, but Chandler still refused to surrender. Instead he was trying to draw his own weapon when Captain Newman jumped into the game and grabbed the negro. Seeing that it was all over, Chandler then submitted to arrest. He was taken to Sevierville and put in jail there.

The scuffle caused considerable stir on the boat, but all who witnessed it say that Captain Newman averted a tragedy as Deputy Davis would certainly have killed his man as soon as Chandler drew his gun. The pistol taken from the negro was a Smith & Wesson of 44 calibre. He will be prosecuted for carrying a pistol and resisting an officer.

For the past seven months Chandler has been in Knoxville, although he belongs in Sevierville which place he left some months ago owing to some trouble which he got into.

Deputy Davis is the same Sevier county officer who took such an important part in the recent Whaley murder case.

DEPUTY'S DANGER

DESPERATE STRUGGLE YESTER-DAY ON THE "TELEPHONE."

Before a Negro Could be Arrested and Disarmed—He is Now in Jail.

Special to The Sentinel.

SEVIERVILLE, Tenn., Feb. 19.—A lively fight, which came near ending in a man being killed, occurred on the steamer Telephone yesterday as that boat was making her regular trip up the river from Knoxville to this place. All went well on the boat until about noon, when a negro named Luther Chandler went to the cook, Sam Patterson, also a negro, and told him that he wanted a lunch. This he secured and after eating it refused to pay for it, saying that he had already paid once and did not propose to pay for anything twice. In the argument which resulted, Chandler called the cook a liar. When the cook started to get something to hit him with, Chandler pulled a 44-calibre Smith & Wesson revolver, but before he could use it the cook had disappeared. Deputy Sheriff Tom Davis, of this county, who was on the boat, was notified of the affair and immediately proceeded to arrest Chandler. The negro resisted desperately and the officer placed his pistol against his breast. Nothing daunted, the negro tried to get his gun out of his pocket and a desperate fight ensued. At this time Captain Newman took a hand in the affair and Chandler was soon under arrest. Had not Captain Newman taken a hand there would have been a dead negro on the boat, for the deputy would have killed him before he would have allowed him to draw his pistol. Upon the arrival of the boat here about dark Chandler was taken before Judge Cox, chairman of the county court, and tried on two charges—carrying a pistol and resisting an officer. He was placed under a heavy bond and being unable to furnish it, was sent to jail. Chandler is considered a desperate character. He had some trouble in Sevier county about a year ago and had been living since then in Knoxville. During the trial Sheriff Maples and other prominent citizens of Sevierville testified as to his bad character.

144

The Whaley murders were not the kind of attention the White Caps needed or wanted, at least not the ones who still adhered to the initial principle of elevating Sevier County's moral quotient by chasing off the prostitutes and punishing adulteresses—and sometimes their clients and paramours. A sense of lawlessness and paranoia pervaded the county, to the extent that some citizens decided they needed legislative support to clean up the mess that law enforcement and courts apparently could not.

On March 17, 1897, Sevier County's grand jury finally heard the evidence against Wynn, Tipton, Catlett and Wade—and found true bills against Tipton and Wynn for murder, and against Catlett and Wade for accessories in the same crime. It's worth noting, again, that John Sam Springs was the jury foreman on that grand jury.

Wynn and Tipton were immediately arrested again. Wade, according to records, was still in custody.

When Catlett heard that his paid assassins had been arrested again, he fled Sevierville for home, six miles out of town. As darkness approached, Davis and Deputy B. A. Rolen also headed that way to apprehend Catlett. They found the Catlett house surrounded by a high wire fence and protected by two bulldogs. Still on their mounts, Davis and Rolen called to the house for Catlett to surrender, but there was no response. The deputies got off their horses, drew their side arms and warily entered the enclosure. The dogs came running at the officers at the gate, then circled them a couple of times but did not attack.

Mary Ann Wade Catlett came to the door, and Davis and Rolen told her Catlett needed to surrender, and if he didn't there would be trouble.

"Bob will never come out," she shouted and slammed the door. The deputies then forced the door open, at which point Catlett shouted from an upstairs room that he would come down to be taken into custody. Arrested and handcuffed again, Bob Catlett, Davis and Rolen began their trip back to Sevierville.

Even before Davis and Rolen could bring in their captive, and in an apparent act of revenge, William Wynn assaulted and badly beat J. D. Davis, the respected father of the deputy. Wynn was eventually tried and convicted for the brutal assault of the elder Davis. The sentence was upheld by the supreme court,[99] and he served a sentence at the county workhouse, that place at which he had previously served as superintendent.

In the immediate aftermath of William Wynn's assault on J. D. Davis, a courier was sent to Deputy Davis, informing him that the White Caps were planning to intercept Davis and Rolen on their ride back to Sevierville and free Catlett from their custody. Deputy Sheriff Davis summoned men to guard Catlett, then departed for Catlettsburg, where he hoped to phone in reinforcements from Sevierville, Knoxville, Dandridge and Strawberry Plains. When he found the phone lines had been cut, Davis then dispatched couriers himself, rallying friends of the Davises. Sensing an armed conflict was all but inevitable, they began gathering all the guns, ammunition and willing associates they could find in response to the plan. A growing number of White Caps—presumably unmasked—were assembling on the courthouse lawn.

Sheriff Maples deputized all the supporters he could find and, leaving a small contingent on guard at the courthouse, rode out to meet Davis, Rolen and Catlett and escort them back to the jail. They linked up near Catlettsburg. On hearing of the plan, Davis rode off across the Little Pigeon River to recruit several more men to the posse. That done, he gave orders to fight to the last, if necessary, and they resumed their journey to Sevierville.

With the area around the courthouse now occupied by armed White Caps, Davis rode into town at the head of the group of armed men, including Sheriff Maples and Deputy Rolen, guarding Catlett. The two groups stared each other down in suspicion and scorn. But the guns remained holstered, and Catlett joined his co-conspirators in jail.

Fearful that an armed conflict was imminent, Sevier County officials hustled the defendants into a courtroom that Saturday night for a bond hearing before Judge W. R. Hicks. Davis stood by inside the courtroom with a shotgun at the ready, in case the standoff were to erupt into violence.

Bloodshed was avoided, but Hicks, whose rulings from the bench were now being questioned as too accommodating to defendants, freed all the suspects in the Whaley murders on bond. No matter how heinous the crime they were accused of, they were out again.

To many of Sevier County's political and economic leaders, the normal legal system seemed incapable of restoring what the U.S. Constitution calls Domestic Tranquility. There were too few arrests, too few prosecutions, too few convictions. Some of those who possessed a measure of influence decided that legislative action on two fronts would be required if the county were to be brought under control again.

Sevier County had been ruled by Justices of the Peace, who had done the bidding of some of the most prominent landowners for the better part of the 1890s, and extraordinary measures would be needed to eradicate the infestation.

And help was on the way, but not without resistance.

19

A Battle for the Heart and Soul of Sevier County

Because Whitecapping had metastasized to the degree it had, radical measures would be necessary to eradicate the cancer—translation: Sevier County was not capable of solving Sevier County's White Cap problem. The collusion, corruption and organized crime was so complete that it altered the very DNA of the county. One of the more vocal opponents of seeking outside assistance in eradicating the White Caps from Sevier County was William Montgomery, "the white-cap editor of the Sevierville Vindicator."[100]

We don't know whether Montgomery was a White Cap or not—had taken the oath or not—but his editorials sometimes suggested he supported extralegal activities when it came to dealing with criminals.

"The STAR does not endorse mob law in any shape, form or fashion, but there ought to be some means provided for the legal execution without judge, jury, clergy or ceremony, of all

---

[100] *Morristown Republican*, Morristown, Tennessee, Saturday, September 30, 1899

villains who invade the sanctity and destroy the happiness of other people's homes."[101]

William Montgomery was born in Sevier County on February 14, 1863, and was the oldest of thirteen children of Capt. Robert Aiken Montgomery and Elizabeth McMahan Montgomery. His early education was accomplished at Porter Academy in Blount County and the Nancy Academy in Sevierville.

He began his career as a school teacher, then later became a book agent. In 1895 he began his journalism career, when he published the Sevierville Star for two years for a stock company. He left the position, *because of political differences* with the owners, and began publishing the Montgomery Vindicator in 1897.

The Vindicator's new motto spoke volumes about a very strong sentiment in Sevier County: Devoted to the Defense of Sevier County Against Robbers at Home and Slanderers Abroad.

Montgomery was never shy about weighing in on matters in Sevier County. A fire had destroyed the old courthouse in 1856, and some of the county's wealthier men were lobbying the county court, made up of Justices of the Peace, against building a new courthouse. Montgomery often referred to these wealthy men as "inflooncers," and it is interesting that these "inflooncers" were opposed to a more modern building. In this instance, though, Montgomery's position on Whitecapping is a little more ambiguous, since he believed the justices had taken longer to act than was necessary. He rather sarcastically suggested another way the county commissioners could save money.[102]

"We understand that Cogdill shoveled his way out with a shovel which had been taken into the jail by Frank M. Woody, an

[101] *Sevierville Star*, May 24, 1895
[102] Cummings, 30

employee of the jailer. If the prisoners are permitted to tear out of jail every week we would suggest that in order to save money and reduce expenses, the court tear down the jail and turn the convicts over to the 'white caps.'"

After the Whaley killings, the movement in Sevier County to end Whitecapping had found traction, and then momentum. The alliance that would finally put an end to it had actually begun in 1894, when Republican Millard Fillmore Maples had been elected High Sheriff, and appointed Democrat Tom Davis as a Deputy Sheriff.

Some folks called this alliance The Law and Order League.

The Law and Order League was made up of Maples, Davis, physician and Whitecap opponent Dr. Z. D. Massey, and the attorney J. R. Penland.

It's interesting to note, that in the battle for the heart and soul of Sevier County, the Law and Order League recognized "the necessity of having its own voice in Sevier County, started its own newspaper, and continued using the name, the Sevierville Star. For a small mountain community to have two local newspapers during this time is indicative of the stress and turmoil caused by the collapse of community in Sevier County."[103]

Realizing justice would never be served while Sevier County remained status quo, they began developing relationships outside Sevier County, particularly in Knox County, that would bolster their credibility and enable them to defeat Whitecapping in Sevier County once and for all. Maples and Davis weren't the only influential citizens who recognized

---

[103] Cummings, 83-84

the need to eliminate the White Caps influence over Sevier County's courts. Adding to his enigmatic role the saga, even Montgomery recognized the source of the corruption.

"The organization of the white caps is the outgrowth of officers [justices of the peace] failing to enforce the law, [by] prohibiting certain habits against some gentlemen ? [sic] who stand high in political and social circles."[104]

The balance of power was beginning to shift in Sevier County, from the Justices of the Peace and their "gangs of White Caps," to the rule of law as dictated by the Tennessee State Legislature.

---

[104] Cummings, 73

20

The Tables, Turned

The first legislative initiative was to pass a new state law designed to specifically address the concept that was at the core of the White Cap phenomenon. It was even called the anti-White Cap law by some, though in the legislation neither that organization nor Grave Yard Hosts nor any other was referred to by name. The law comprised multiple provisions, but the first three were most pertinent:

Section 1 made it a felony to enter into a conspiracy between two or more people to take a human life or to administer corporal punishment— such as a withe whipping—or to burn, destroy or seize the victim's property. Conviction of such an offense could result in a prison sentence of between three and twenty-one years. That sentence would be in addition to any conviction for the actual assault or killing.

Section 2 provided the same punishment for anyone who procured or encouraged another individual to become a part of such a conspiracy.

Section 3 was the provision that made the whole law workable, at least in Sevier County. It said that anyone convicted of any act covered in the first two sections would be prohibited from sitting on any trial or grand jury, and made it the duty of the court to exclude them. Furthermore, if any suspicion arose about a prospective or seated juror having even participated in any such activity, the court was instructed to immediately look into the matter, calling witnesses if necessary, and to dismiss anyone "shown to be implicated" in the offenses.

Certainly the law covered not just the White Capping, but also others. However, its passage in the 1897 legislative session was directly focused on solving Sevier County's White Cap problem, and that law, combined with another, was viewed by county power brokers as a new and useful instrument with which to eviscerate the White Caps.

From the other side of the issue, members of the White Caps, particularly those whose affiliation was common knowledge, had a new fearsome issue to deal with. Now something as simple as jury duty could be dangerous, potentially exposing the organization. So White Caps began to routinely seek exemption from juries, feigning illness or even sending a proxy in their place, so the eyes of the court would not turn on them.

Responsibility for the second piece of legislation fell on the shoulders of Tom Davis.

On the Monday after the Whaley defendants bonded out, Tom Davis, in service to these leaders and his county, boarded a train at Strawberry Plains, headed for Nashville to meet with members of the Tennessee General Assembly. He carried with him a request to realign the criminal court of Sevier County in such a way that Judge Hicks, in whom the county power structure had lost confidence, would no longer be presiding over White Cap cases. Hicks's honesty or allegiances were not in question as much as his courage and toughness in demanding justice and handing down sentences with teeth in them.

County leaders prevailed on the legislature to reassign Sevier County's criminal court jurisdiction from the Second Judicial Circuit Court under Judge Hicks to the Knoxville district under the hand and gavel of Judge Thomas Amos Rogers Nelson, Jr.. Judge Nelson was a much more authoritative jurist, not known to be beholden to any individual or group, nor to hold back when it came time to confront criminals with their misdeeds and see that they paid the price for them.

G.W. Pickle, the state's attorney general who had already successfully defended Tennessee in a border dispute with Virginia, drew up the bill, which was introduced by State Sen. Horace Atlee "Mystery" Mann and supported by his fellow Knox County legislator, Sen. John C. Houk, a former congressman. Opposition to the court realignment was led by Sen. Lucian C. Keeney of Campbell County, who characterized the issue as a personal fight between Davis and Judge Hicks. Judge Nelson, Keeney said, should not be forced on an unwilling population in Sevier County. Newspaper articles, at times comically, elaborated on the spat between Knox and Sevier Counties, and their respective supporters.

Davis, with time in the legislative session running short, returned to Sevier the following Monday without having gained passage of the bill. But it so happened that that Monday was the day the Sevier County Court, the legislative body, was scheduled to meet. During a 1:00 session, Davis told the court what had transpired in Nashville and asked the members for a resolution in support of the bill that he could show legislators.

The resolution passed unanimously, and with that document in hand, Davis mounted his favorite horse and dashed back the 27 miles to Knoxville, where he caught another train to Nashville. The next morning, Tuesday, Davis was on hand when the Tennessee General Assembly was gaveled into session. He presented the unanimous resolution to the legislature, swaying enough votes for passage. Hicks never again presided over court in Sevier County.

SEVIERVILLE STAR
SCINTILLATIONS.

Dr. J. J. Ellis left for Knoxville and other "pints" Sunday on an "inflooencen" expedition.

—

J. F. Shults and family moved to Knoxville last week. Mr. Shults did not go for the purpose of seeking the protection of the Journal and Tribune nor for the purpose of avoding assassination, yet our gain is Knoxville's loss.

—

E. E. Houk, a prominent Knoxville attorney came up Friday and remained until Saturday afternoon. He came up not to practice law, but to hunt ducks and recreate. He had along the duck-boat in which Hon. John C. Houk was defeated for congress in 1894. He took back with him a good sized "Ketch" (Judge Hicks, Gen. Henderson and A. F. Bryan). The sensational reporters of the Journal and Tribune were wonderfully surprised that he could visit Sevierville and return alive. Come again. L.

—

Judge Nelson could clean out the white caps of Sevier county if he were on the bench.—Knoxville Sentinel.

I will bet a quarter of a dollar against a half pint of mean whiskey that if Sevier county is transferred to the circuit of Nelson and Mynatt, both will join the white caps during their first court at Sevierville.—An "inflooencer" who knows. We can't see where anything is to be gained; W. R. Hicks is our judge at present, but the Knoxville papers try us and we presume would do so if we were in Judge Nelson's circuit.

—

Ben. Sewell, of Loudon county, was found dead on his father's porch last Saturday morning with 35 holes in his head and breast. According to the Knoxville press, Sewell with a band of white caps visited an old man the night before, when the old man gave them the contents of his gun the whole load taking effect in Sewell. But as the Knoxville papers never tell the truth about Sevier county we presume they treat other counties the same way.

———

Seventy million people know Hood's Sarsaparilla purifies the blood, strengthens the system and gives good health.

"Sevierville Star Scintillations" The editor of the Sevierville Star, W. R. Montgomery, was so opposed to the judicial jurisdiction swap that he left the Star and started publishing The Sevierville Vindicator. Montgomery clearly had issues with the Knoxville press.

The anti-White Cap law would not be signed by the governor until the following spring, but Judge T. A. R. Nelson, Jr., had a copy of it in his breast pocket when he strode to the bench on his first day presiding over a Sevier County court in July 1897.

CHAPTER 52.

[SENATE BILL NO. 368.]

AN ACT to prevent and punish the formation or continuance of conspiracies and combinations of persons for certain unlawful purposes, and to declare the punishment and the methods of inflicting it, and the disqualifications of persons who shall become or remain members of such conspiracies and combinations ; and of persons who shall directly or indirectly encourage or procure others to become or remain members thereof ; and of persons who shall directly or indirectly aid, abet or encourage any of the schemes or purposes of such unlawful conspiracies or combinations.

Conspiracy a felony. Section 1. *Be it enacted by the General Assembly of the State of Tennessee,* That it shall be a felony punishable by from three to twenty-one years imprisonment in the penitentiary and by full judgment of infamy and disqualification, for two or more persons to enter into or form any conspiracy or combination, or to remain in any conspiracy or combination under any name, or upon any pretext whatsoever, to take human life, or to engage in any act reasonably calculating to cause the loss of life, whether generally or of a class or classes, or of any individual or individuals; or to inflict corporal punishment or injury, whether generally or upon a class or classes, or upon an individual or individuals; or to burn or otherwise destroy property or to feloniously take the same, whether generally or of a class or classes or of an individual or individuals.

Encouraging unlawful conspiracy a felony. Sec. 2. *Be it further enacted,* That it shall be a felony, punished in like manner as the offense described in the first Section of this Act, for any person, either directly or indirectly to procure or encourage anyone to become or remain a member of any such unlawful conspiracy or combination as is described in the first Section of this Act; or for any person either directly or indirectly to aid, abet, or encourage any person to engage or remain in such conspiracies or combinations or to aid or abet in the accomplishment of any purpose or end of such conspiracies or combinations.

Senate Bill No. 368, also known unofficially as
"The Anti-White Cap Bill"

Sec. 3. *Be it further enacted,* That no person who has been guilty of any offense declared in the two preceding Sections of this Act shall be competent to sit or serve on any grand or traverse jury, and it shall be the duty of the court to carefully exclude all such persons from the juries, both grand and petit; and when he shall be informed or shall have reason to suspect any person presented as a juror guilty of any of said offenses, he shall call witnesses, if necessary, and examine fully into the truth of the charge; he shall dismiss from the grand jury any person who has been selected and afterwards shown to be implicated in any of said offenses. *Offenders incompetent to serve as jurors.*

Sec. 4. *Be it further enacted,* That the judges of the criminal and circuit courts shall give this Act specially in charge to grand juries, and the grand juries shall have inquisitorial power of the offenses herein declared. *Inquisitorial powers.*

Sec. 5. *Be it further enacted,* That indictments framed under this Act shall not be held insufficient by reason of the general nature of the charges preferred, or for embracing more than one of said offenses in the same indictment.

Sec. 6. *Be it further enacted,* That this Act take effect from and after its passage, the public welfare requiring it.

Passed March 22, 1897.

JOHN THOMPSON,
Speaker of the Senate.

MORGAN C. FITZPATRICK,
Speaker of the House of Representatives.

Approved March 24, 1897.

ROBT. L. TAYLOR,
Governor.

Senate Bill No. 368, also known unofficially as
"The Anti-White Cap Bill"

CHAPTER 223.

[HOUSE BILL No. 738.]

AN ACT to detach Sevier County from the Second Judicial Circuit and transfer and attach it to the criminal district composed of Knox County, and to provide for the holding of the terms of the Circuit Court of the county of Sevier.

Change of judicial circuits Section 1. *Be it enacted by the General Assembly of the State of Tennessee,* That the county of Sevier be and the same is detached from the second judicial circuit and transferred and attached to the criminal district composed of Knox County.

Duty of judge. Sec. 2. *Be it further enacted,* That it shall be the duty of the judge of the "criminal court for the district of Knox County," to hold the terms of the circuit court of said county of Sevier, and he is invested with full power and jurisdiction to do so.

Duty of district attorney Sec. 3. *Be it further enacted,* That it shall be the duty of the district attorney for the criminal district composed of Knox County to attend the terms of the circuit court of Sevier County, and perform in and for said court all duties imposed by law upon district attorneys of this State.

—531—

Sec. 4. *Be it further enacted,* That this Act take effect from and after its passage, the public welfare requiring it.

Passed April 7, 1897.

MORGAN C. FITZPATRICK,
Speaker of the House of Representatives.

JOHN THOMPSON,
Speaker of the Senate.

Approved April 8, 1897.

ROBT. L. TAYLOR,
Governor.

House Bill No. 738, Legislation moving
Sevier County judicial jurisdiction to Knox County.

Judge Nelson was accompanied by Knox County Attorney General E. Fred Mynatt in July 1897.

Nelson was the fifth of 11 children born to the man he shared a name with. The elder Nelson was a famed East Tennessee attorney from Roane County—a staunch Unionist during the Civil War. He was elected twice to Congress, but as he was traveling to Washington to begin his second term in 1861, he was captured by Confederate forces in Kentucky and jailed in Richmond, Virginia. He was ordered released by Confederate President Jefferson Davis on promising not to actively oppose the southern government. He also served on the defense team during the impeachment trial of President Andrew Johnson, and as a Tennessee Supreme Court justice.

The younger Nelson's legal career is not nearly so well-documented, except through his reputation, which was one of toughness. That there was little further biographical data on him could simply be evidence of a legal life that was uncontroversial because it was generally considered straight up and beyond reproach. He had about him an air of dignity and determination that was bound to have gotten the attention of Sevier County's White Caps, particularly when, after charging his first grand jury in that sweltering July courtroom, he pulled out the copy of the new law and read it to them.

The courtroom was jammed with spectators, who wanted to know whether Nelson would be as direct as his reputation indicated. Even in that sweaty room, Nelson seemed cool and deliberate as he read the law, and then, so there would be no misunderstanding, he elaborated on what it meant and the issue it was meant to address. It was the first time in several years that White Caps felt uncomfortable in a Sevier County courtroom. A few White Caps made excuses as to why they could not serve on the grand jury, and others were deposed by the judge, who told them in no uncertain terms they were no more eligible to serve than a horse thief.

If the assembled needed any more proof that Nelson had a low tolerance for nonsense, it came within hours. As the sun set in Sevierville that day, a group of about a dozen young "toughs" decided to engage in a little friendly intimidation, probably incited by some segment of the White Caps and emboldened by that unique brand of fearlessness that comes packaged in a bottle with a cork.

The young men gathered in front of the hotel where Judge Nelson and Attorney General Mynatt were staying and repeatedly marched back and forth, singing a loud, raucous and probably off-key rendition of "We will hang Judge Nelson from a sour apple tree …" Sometimes they substituted Mynatt's name for Nelson's.

It was July. The windows were open, so Mynatt and Nelson could not help but hear—and be amused at—the choral performance being staged for their benefit. Nelson summoned Sheriff Maples and had him and his deputies get the names of the choir members and submit them to Mynatt for indictment on nuisance charges and "general cussedness."

Maples appeared at the courthouse the following Monday in the company of the singers, who were fearful that the judge's wrath was about to come crashing down. Nelson delivered a stern and threatening lecture to the men as they stood silent before him. Nelson placed all of them under bond to appear in court at a later date, but that is pretty much where it ended. No further investigation was conducted, and there was no subsequent court action. But there was no more nighttime caroling outside the hotel, either. The only singing that was to come would come from the witness stand

Judge Nelson's early action in Sevierville signaled to everyone that the county had undergone a change of direction, particularly in light of the two new laws on the books that restored credibility to the court system and brought a sense of foreboding to the White Caps. The future of Sevier County and the White Caps looked very different.

The rest of the summer and most of the fall in 1897 was a time of evidence gathering for the prosecution of Wynn and Tipton. Sevier County, particularly Sevierville, remained a tense place, but the explosiveness that surrounded the arrests of the four murder defendants subsided. The trials for the deaths of Bill and Laura Whaley were to be separate, though the ones accused of directly causing their deaths were scheduled to be tried together.

Their court date was set for November 15. A newsworthy event was reported the day before, on November 14, 1898, as Sheriff Tom Davis had gone to great lengths to track down and bring back the two notorious killers, Newt Green and Wes Hendricks.

21

The Manhunt of Newt Green and Wes Hendricks

The pivotal year for the White Caps was 1897. The first few months were consumed in the outrage over the Bill and Laura Whaley murders. But this was also the period during which Tom Davis was hot on the Texas trail of Wes Hendricks and Newt Green in the Aaron McGill killing, and the shootings of McGill's son and son-in-law.

Their second-degree murder convictions in the death of Aaron McGill netted them each a 20-year term in the state prison, even though there was convincing evidence—including the victim's dying declaration—that the killing was premeditated and that there were, beyond question, aggravating circumstances.

Whether their punishment was mitigated at all by the presence of White Caps on the jury or within the courtroom apparatus may never be known. And for that matter, what was the revenue source that allowed these two to appeal their convictions to a higher court? It was while that appeal was pending that Hendricks and Green joined a notorious Knox County outlaw named George Thurmer and other prisoners at the Sevier County Jail in overpowering a jailer and taking his keys. Thurmer grabbed

162

the jailer as he handed the prisoner his breakfast and held him as others grabbed the keys. All escaped, and Green and Hendricks fled into the protective hills outside of Pigeon Forge. Green and Hendricks were tough and had the indigenous mountain shrewdness that was necessary for survival in these hills The two spent several months there, staying with White Cap sympathizers in Little Cove but openly walking the roads and working in the fields in the summer of 1897. Sheriff Maples and his men set many a trap for the duo, but advance knowledge of the plans always seemed to thwart their capture.

Rumors of sightings were widespread, but they apparently felt little threat of being taken back into custody. It also became widely known that the criminals had been assigned to clean up their own mess by assassinating J. R. Penland, who had prosecuted them, Tom Davis and Dr. Z. D. Massey, an unabashed White Cap opponent. But a contact of Massey's alerted the doctor to the plot and it was foiled.

It was about then that something or somebody led them to the conclusion that it was time to disappear, and they did, just ahead of a deputized posse led by Maples and Davis.

Davis then set out on their trail alone, and pursued them through the mountains from Murphy, North Carolina to Blue Ridge, Georgia. He had a close encounter with them in Blue Ridge, but they managed to elude him.

"Tom searched the surrounding by-roads until it was dark, then rode into Blue Ridge to spend the night.

Green and Hendricks, seated on the railroad near by to eat the cold cornbread given them by the old man, dashed behind a little tree when they heard Davis's horse.

'Well, what do you think of that," said Green. "If that ain't Tom Davis I'm a liar. We just got these rabbit feet in time to bring us luck."[105]

Green and Hendricks, having evaded capture in Blue Ridge, Georgia, "crossed the mountains to Tellico Plains, Tenn., sold one of their pistols and an overcoat to go West. They are now in Paris, Texas."[106]

Davis disappeared again; this time headed for Texas. Only Dr. Massey and Davis's brother-in-law, Andrew Love, knew where Davis was going. Disguised as a book agent, Davis made his way to Paris, Texas. There he connected with local law enforcement and enlisted their help in apprehending Green and Hendricks, but they were not there. Shortly thereafter, Davis received a telegram reading, "Your men at Honey Grove—Z. D. Massey."

Honey Grove, in Fannin County, was a pencil dot of a town in northeast Texas about 30 miles west of Paris, which is in neighboring Lamar County. By sunset Davis was in Honey Grove. Again, Davis called upon local lawmen to help with his chase, and they joined the hunt. They scratched the earth all around Honey Grove but could not dig Green and Hendricks out. But they had been seen. The duo had vanished again, hopping a freight train in Honey Grove headed east.

Davis got another telegram: "Your men at New Boston, going by the names of Frank Nolan and Charlie Harrison—Z. D. Massey."

The last passenger train to New Boston had already left Honey Grove by the time Davis got his wire, so he tried to board a freight car himself. But a member of the train's crew refused to let Davis ride, telling him he was new to the job because his predecessor was fired for letting two men get on the train to New Boston a few nights earlier. "Where is that man?" Davis asked. He tracked down the now-unemployed man, who provided

---

[105] Yadon, *Knoxville News-Sentinel*, June 2, 1929
[106] Ibid

a description of the freight-jumpers that matched that of the fugitives. The trail was getting warmer.

The next morning Davis was at the train depot long before the train to New Boston chugged into town. The deputy boarded the train and rumbled toward the last known location of Green and Hendricks. Davis was met at New Boston by Bowie County Deputy Ed Lynch, but the fugitives were still a couple of steps ahead of their pursuers and had vacated New Boston. Davis and Lynch conducted an intense search of the area but again came up empty. They had vanished without a trace.

His quest at a dead end, Davis began making preparations to return to East Tennessee. Davis had been chasing Green and Hendricks for months, and about to head home empty-handed, Davis was waiting at the train station with Deputy Lynch when a cattle trader rode into town. Lynch said, "There goes a man who has been all over eastern Texas buying cattle. And he never forgets a face." Questioned about Green and Hendricks, the man said he did see them 11 miles away, headed toward "Indian Territory," which within a decade would become Oklahoma.

Bowie County was in the northeast corner of Texas, at the point where it, Louisiana and Arkansas all come together. Texarkana shares Bowie County with New Boston. Davis was getting closer.

Wasting no time, Davis, Lynch and the cattle buyer were off in a hack toward their prey.

At the Red River they met an old black man and asked him about Green and Hendricks. He told them, "Yassah, boss, I'll tell you. They're right over in that cotton gin right now."

Davis and Lynch crossed the Red River and split up to cover the exits of the cotton gin.

Green was the first to be apprehended, Lynch telling him he was wanted in Texarkana. But Green knew better.

"Hell, I've heard that tale before. We ain't done nothin' in Texarkana.

"I'm guessing, by God, Tom Davis wants us in Tennessee."

Green glanced to the side and said, "Hello, Tom. By God, you've got your mustache blacked, but I know you."

Hendricks was arrested without much fanfare shortly thereafter, and now Davis finally got to make use of his handcuffs, handcuffing Green and Hendricks to each other. On the trip back to New Boston, the captives were heard to sing, "Take me back to Tennessee/There let me live and die."

One fascinating account of where Dr. Massey was getting his information on the movements of Green and Hendricks, which he telegraphed to Davis during the Texas excursion, suggests Dr. Z. D. Massey had befriended a White Cap, because Dr. Massey had once saved his life by an operation.[107] Sheriff Davis nicknamed this unknown mole, who had entered into a hog-raising partnership with Green's and Hendricks' girlfriends' father, "Jap." It seems "Jap" was "an expert at cards and an expert in telling fortunes," and evidently he used this skill.to elicit the whereabouts of Green and Hendricks from their unsuspecting girlfriends.

Deputy Sheriff Tom Davis, center, brings fugitive killers Newt Green, left, and Wes Hendricks back to Sevierville handcuffed together.

Photo courtesy of Carroll McMahan

The Tennessee Supreme Court in November 1898 affirmed the convictions and 20-year sentences of Green and Hendricks in the murder of Aaron McGill. They were the only two White Caps to spend time in prison for their activities.

---

[107] Yadon, *The Knoxville News-Sentinel*, June 2, 1929

An interesting twist in the Green and Hendricks saga was related to us by Tim Fisher, the Sevier County genealogist at the King Family Library in Sevierville. Newspaper reports say that Green and Hendricks were sentenced to the Brushy Mountain Penitentiary, and not long after they arrived "Hendricks was killed at the prison by falling slate, and Green was afterward pardoned."[108]

According to Fisher, Hendricks paid a visit to see his aunt *after* his death was reported, gathered up his belongings and was never seen or heard from again, suggesting he faked his own death by substituting another inmate's body for his own.

The capture of Green and Hendricks created quite a stir, as they were notorious fugitives who had been doggedly pursued and captured by Deputy Sheriff Tom Davis.

With Green and Hendricks back in custody, the trial of James Catlett Tipton and Pleasant D. Wynn was again the talk of the town.

---

[108] MAN WHO BROKE UP WHITE CAPS DIES, *The Knoxville News-Sentinel*, August 3, 1930

22

Going Courting

It is eerily ironic that a brutal double-murder was the incident that broke the stranglehold the White Caps had on Sevier County. No one knew it then, but when Bill and Laura Whaley died, so did the White Caps' influence over Sevier county.

In the outrage that followed the killings, the White Caps lost control over law enforcement and the court system, and consequently they lost what gave them their strength—the fear they were able to plant in the hearts of average people. Members of the organization, once arrogant and prideful of their affiliation, now attempted to suppress any outward connection that might implicate them in the Whaley murders.

For eight months, from the March indictment of Wynn, Tipton, Catlett and Wade until their trials began in November, Sevier County waited, whispered, and waited some more for an anticipated new act of White Cap retribution or more indictments. The only certainty about the future was that two local boys were about to experience justice in a fashion that had been unthinkable eight months earlier.

In order to empanel anything close to an impartial jury, Sevier County had to summon 1,200 men from which to choose twelve to actually hear the case of the *State of Tennessee v. Pleasant D. Wynn and James Catlett Tipton* on charges of murder in the first degree in the death of Laura McMahan Whaley.[109]

With the help of Kyle Hovious, a Digital Specialist with the Special Collections Department at the University of Tennessee's Hodges Library, and Kyle Perkins of RoseWood Virtual Tours, we were able to access and take photographs of the Donald F. Paine Collection. This was a virtual gold mine, in which we found the transcripts from the first Tipton and Wynn murder trial in November 1897, which we've already cited a number of times.

Of course the two defendants, James Catlett Tipton and Pleasant D. Wynn declared their innocence. But by reading the testimony of all of the witnesses and the defendants, a clearer picture of the character (or lack of) of the witnesses emerged—evidence that they truly were a Brood of Vipers and Den of Thieves. Bob Catlett and Bob Wade also testified, and denied any involvement with the Whaley killings and the rocking and shooting of Walter Maples' cabin.

With Judge T. A. R. Nelson, Jr., presiding, the prosecution was handled by an all-star team comprising E. Fred. Mynatt, James Royal "J. R." Penland, W. A. Parton and former U.S. Rep. John C. Houk. The defense team was equally stellar in reputation, though it is unclear whether they were on the payroll of someone with cash to spare or simply wanted to be part of arguably the highest profile criminal case in the history of the county. They were Colonel W. J. McSween, George L. Zirkle and Captain W. M. Mullendore, among others. This cast of luminaries only intensified the public focus on the case, with the lawyers in the courtroom outnumbering the defendants by more than 4-1. The case was on the docket for November 15, 1897—322 days after the Whaleys were killed.

---

[109] Between 650 and 1500 men were believed to have been White Caps. There were about 4,000 registered voters (all male) in Sevier County.

Jury selection consumed five days, as prosecutors tried to weed current and former White Caps and their sympathizers out of the jury box. Attorneys on both sides heavily interrogated potential jurors, trying to find men who had not yet formed an opinion on the guilt or innocence of Wynn and Tipton.

In Sevier County, that was not easy, but on November 19, 1897, the jury was seated.

"The jury was secured at ten o'clock and stands as follows: Sam Russell, W. C. Cate, W. B. Johnson, T. R. Randles, I. A. Hatcher, William Fisk, Joe Allen, J. G. Edwards, Jasper Webb, Calvin Breeden, Baxter Nolan and Albert Whittaker."[110]

Security was tight at the packed courthouse as the prosecution began calling a parade of witnesses to the stand. Not surprisingly, the key testimony came from Lizzie Chandler, Laura Whaley's sister and as close to an eyewitness as there was. She recounted to a captivated courtroom how the killers had burst into the Whaley cabin without warning, how Bill Whaley had begged for their lives, how Laura Whaley had kissed her six-week-old baby, Molly, and how she handed the child over to Lizzie in the full knowledge that she was about to die an unmerciful death at the hand of someone whose face she would not see.

When Lizzie was asked by prosecution attorneys if she recognized anyone in the courtroom as having been one of the two armed intruders responsible for the death of her sister and brother-in-law, she hesitated as spectators and court officers breathlessly awaited her answer. Finally, her gaze fell on Wynn. The tense silence lingered for a moment, and then she looked at Judge Nelson, who asked her, "Have you found him?"

"Yes," she answered.

Attorney General Mynatt asked, "Where is he?"

---

[110] SHE SWEARS THE MAN WAS PLEAS WYNNE, *The Knoxville Tribune*, November 20, 1897

"There," she witness pointed at Wynn and issued a sworn, affirmative identification. "He is the man who had the gun on the night of the murder." No equivocation. No reasonable doubt.

It would have been hard for an honest jury to get around that kind of testimony. Lizzie Chandler had placed Pleas Wynn in the room when and where Laura Whaley was shot to death and with a gun in his hand. Little more needed to be said.

Not so, however, in the case of J. C. Tipton. She could not identify him as definitively as she had Wynn. Having neither seen any portion of his face nor heard his voice, she could only offer a description of the second killer by size and stature. And Laura Whaley, as a protective measure, had pulled bedclothes over Lizzie's face and that of the baby, so that Lizzie had not actually seen that it was Tipton, not Wynn, who had fired the fatal shots.

Prosecutors knew that and did not produce much evidence that would convict Tipton in this case. But they did elicit testimony from Tipton on the witness stand that, though he was not complicit in the killings, he had been with Wynn on the night of the murders. The prosecutors also knew, with that admission, they would get another crack at convicting him at the defendants' second trial, for the murder of Bill Whaley.

In Chapter One we included the confessions of James Catlett Tipton and Pleas Wynn, and both said they were guilty, but had been convicted based on perjured testimony.

We have labeled what the White Caps eventually became a Brood of Vipers and Den of Thieves, and as one might imagine, there should always be suspicion when those of like and disreputable character accuse one another. Oftentimes during the testimony, when asked about the general character of a number of witnesses, a common response was, "I am acquainted with his general character. It is bad. He is not entitled to full faith and credit on oath."[111]

The man who stated that Pleas Wynn confessed to him that he had killed the Whaleys was none other than Sam Jenkins, who was under the sentence of manslaughter for the killing of Ellen Deats. Jake Jenkins testified that Pleas Wynn "was at his house and got a 38-caliber pistol and a bottle of whiskey."[112]

Bob Catlett and Bob Wade were not on trial, however, one witness claimed to have overheard Robert Catlett offer Pleas Wynn money to keep them from testifying against him. .

> "I know defendant Pleas Wynn, and I know Robert Catlett, who is indicted in this case. I remember hearing Robert Catlett tell defendant Wynn he would Two hundred dollars to keep William Whaley and wife from being witnesses against him any more, and Pleas Wynn said he would take it. This conversation occurred at the printing office about a week before the killing of the Whaleys. Catlett and defendant Wynn came out of the Star Office, and Catlett said to him, I would give Two hundred dollars to keep the Whaleys from being witnesses against me" and deft. Wynn said, "I'll take it."

> Under cross-examination Bailey stated: This conversation took place at William Montgomery's printing office, opposite Mrs. Mitchell's here in Sevierville. Catlett and defendant Wynn saw me there, they just walked on. They were talking where I could hear them."[113]

---

[111] PLEAS WYNN V, STATE, TRIAL I
[112] SHE SWEARS THE MAN WAS PLEAS WYNNE, *The Knoxville Tribune*, November 20, 1897
[113] William Bailey testimony, PLEAS WYNN V. STATE, TRIAL I

Another unexpected twist in the trial occurred when it was learned that the mother of William and John Whaley had died and was secretly buried. This left a hole in the prosecution, and it was expected that the defense would make the case that it was John Whaley who had killed his brother Bill and sister-in-law Laura. This led to speculation that friends of Tipton's and Wynn's put her out of the way, which it was believed would lead to another investigation.[114]

The defense team in this trial did its best to impugn the character of Lizzie Chandler by introducing charges made by her husband, John, in their divorce case.[115] But that did not carry their case for acquittal very far. Testimony in the trial lasted four days, with the courtroom jammed every session. Lizzie produced a certificate of divorce which had been granted on the grounds of adultery. That completed, the attorneys prepared their final arguments.

Laura Whaley's parents, Blackburn and Susan McMahan, and Lizzie Chandler and the baby, Mollie Lillard Whaley, all stayed in Sevierville's Snapp Hotel during the trial. Prosecutor Mynatt occupied a room that adjoined the McMahans'. In the quiet of the evening, with only a thin wall separating them, Mynatt did not have to strain much to overhear Blackburn McMahan's lengthy and strident prayer for his daughter's soul, and the cooing of the orphaned baby on the night before his final argument.

McMahan reminded the Lord in his own way of Laura's character and sweetness, and in a voice that quivered with emotion he beseeched his God to deliver justice in that Sevierville courtroom for a young mother whose life was always hard and much too brief.

The words and the emotion that passed easily through the hotel wall that night also penetrated Myatt directly to his core. He was moved by the

---

[114] SHE SWEARS THE MAN WAS PLEAS WYNNE, *The Knoxville Tribune*, November 20, 1897
[115] Crozier, 138

family's abiding pain at the loss of their daughter in such a horrendous way, and was inspired by their faith and gentleness. The episode, it was said, was the wellspring from which flowed a most eloquent and persuasive appeal to the Sevier County jury to hold the two defendants accountable for their barbarous act. It was an attempt to touch the jurors' sensitivities the way his own had been.

Mynatt, too, recounted for the overcrowded courtroom the burdens of Laura Whaley's life, the circumstances of her death, and he punctuated his oratory with the images that had been imprinted on his mind by Blackburn McMahan's sorrowful prayer. Many a tear had been brushed away by the time Mynatt's address ended at dusk on November 24, the day before Thanksgiving 1897.

Judge Nelson gave his charge to the jury by candlelight, and the jury retired that night to begin deliberations.

Pleas Wynn had precious little to be thankful for the next day, when a verdict of guilty was returned for him in the death of Laura Whaley.

"It is therefore considered by the Court, that the defendant Pleas Wynn for the offence of Murder in the first degree of which he stands convicted, shall be for satisfactory reasons sent to the jail of Knox County, in there be kept in close confinement until Friday the 21st of January, 1898, at which time he will be sent back to Sevier County, when between the hours of Ten o'clock A. M. and four o'clock P. M. upon a gallows erected within the prison walls. Or an enclosure adjacent thereto, erected as to exclude the public view, the Sheriff of Sevier County or some of his legally appointed deputies, shall hang the defendant Pleas Wynn by the neck until he is dead."[116]

[116] PLEAS WYNN V. STATE, TRIAL I

J. C. Tipton was acquitted but was held on $10,000 bond in preparation for his and Wynn's trial in the killing of Bill Whaley.

As he sat in his cell for the next few months, Wynn must have wondered if he alone would be tagged with responsibility for the murders, all because his White Cap hood had slipped away from the side of his face momentarily in the bright light of the Whaley's humble hearth. And he had not even fired the fatal shots.

As the spring term of Sevier County's circuit court approached, the public fever again began to rise, because Pleas Wynn and J. C. Tipton were to go on trial again, this time in the murder of Bill Whaley. Most everyone knew this would not be the end of the narrative, just one more milepost on the journey. Wynn had been convicted, and now the community returned to see if the proceedings would validate the common belief that Tipton, who was acquitted of one murder, was in reality just as guilty as the man who had been convicted.

The trial began April 5, 1898.

The cases for both the prosecution and the defense were essentially re-presentations of the evidence in the Laura Whaley trial. Lizzie Chandler again was the center of attention with her story of horror and sadness. Testimony like that is difficult to counter, if not impossible. In addition, the prosecution entered into evidence the prior testimony of J. C. Tipton that he had been in Wynn's company from sunset to midnight on the day of the Whaley murders. With that admission, how could he not have had a role in the slayings?

But it was not an ardent, overheard prayer and the oratory it inspired that would provide the extra-legal drama for this trial.

Owen Dickey was the final witness for the prosecution, and he testified that in an encounter on the day of the murders, Pleas Wynn had showed him a handful of bullets and said, "When I go a-fishin', I take these along and kill damn big game."

Dickey's testimony angered Wynn's brother, William, who had refused the use of his bloodhounds in the search for a murderer in another case, and had assaulted the aged father of Deputy Tom Davis. William had been drinking all that spring day, and he was one of those people for whom alcohol was the release valve for the darker side of their personality.

When court adjourned, William Wynn "tanked up on bad mountains dew,"[117] confronted Owen Dickey inside the building and began cursing and threatening him and calling him a liar. Responding to the commotion, Sheriff Maples intervened and ordered Wynn out of the courthouse. But then, as the sheriff was walking back to his office, Wynn and a group of his friends stepped out of a livery stable and turned their curses on him. Badly outnumbered and believing his life was at stake, Maples pulled his revolver and opened fire. The sheriff fired five times, and four of the bullets found their way into the belly of William Wynn, mortally wounding him.

The second-term sheriff, now holding a sidearm with an empty cylinder, began to back away from the enraged cohorts of William Wynn and then bolted toward the security of his office nearby. But the crowd was able to cut him off and seize him before he could get there. At that instant Deputy Davis arrived on the scene with his own pistol drawn, and surreptitiously placed a handful of cartridges in the hand of Sheriff Maples, who began to reload his weapon. Also arriving on the scene were Detective C. W. McCall and George Thurmer, a notorious Knox County outlaw whom Davis had captured in Kentucky. Thurmer had turned state's evidence and had been providing law enforcement with intelligence on the White Caps for some time.

---

[117] KILLED AT SEVIERVILLE, *Knoxville Sentinel*, April 7, 1898

BLOODSHED IN SEVIER COUNTY

William Wynn Shot by Sheriff Maples and will Likely Die.

The confrontation was defused with no further bloodshed, but Sheriff Maples immediately appeared before Judge Nelson in connection with the shooting of William Wynn. The judge ordered Maples into the custody of the county and instructed Davis to form a strong guard for Maples' protection.

As Davis headed for the jail with his boss-prisoner, Hagan Bailey, who was William Wynn's brother-in-law and Catlett Tipton's nephew, made an attempt to shoot the sheriff. But before he could get a shot off, Bailey was quickly disarmed and subdued by Detective McCall and then jailed.

The shooting of Wynn by Sheriff Maples further polarized the White Caps and their sympathizers, and those who opposed Whitecapping and were committed to its demise. A battle seemed imminent, as calls were made to both camps to arm themselves and converge on Sevierville.

Before he succumbed to his wounds, Squire Bill Wynn made the following statement:[118]

"Fillmore Maples came along. I asked him if he got Owen Dickey to get out a warrant for me. He said he didn't try. I told him he did try, and I could prove it on him. I told him he was a low-down rascal. I was walking along behind him carrying a bucket of water. I saw him begin to draw his pistol. I just told him he was a low-down rascal and he began shooting. I never

---

[118] BLOODSHED IN SEVIER COUNTY, *The Knoxville Tribune*, April 7, 1898

said anything else to him. He shot me till I fell, and I think he shot me after I fell. I never had any pistol. I never made any attack on him, or did anything to him. I don't know what the result will be. I am suffering awfully. I make this statement in view that I might die.

"Signed,   W. M. Wynn

"Attest—P. Maples, C. W. Cox.

"Sworn to and subscribed before me. This April 6th, 1898

"J. R. HOUK, J. P."

William Wynn died, and some believed he had been the "real leader" of the Sevier County White Caps, and that with his death the driving force behind Whitecapping died as well.

Was William "Bill" Wynn the Chief Mogul of High Cockalorum? The answer to that question will never be confirmed one way or the other, but he is as likely as anyone during the saga to have held that position.

The shooting of William Wynn by Sheriff Maples was just one more inciting incident in a series of inciting incidents, and Sevier Countians were on edge wondering what might happen next.

23

Insurrection Looms

Darkness was typically when the White Caps went about their work, and that was again the case in the hours after William Wynn was gunned down by Sheriff Maples. White Cap couriers went out in every direction from Sevierville intreating all available White Caps to come to town to redress the wrongs being perpetrated on their cohorts by law enforcers, and a community that had lost patience with vigilantism.

Maples, still the sheriff despite being in custody, used a device that did not have a long history in Sevier County to call for help—he telephoned Sheriff Jesse C. Groner of Knox County, Knoxville Police Chief C. A. Reeder and Blount County Sheriff S. A. Walker. Each responded by dispatching a posse of men about 9 p.m. to Sevier County. In Sheriff Groner's posse were Deputies Warnack, Dobson, Meek, Reynolds, Dogan, Shipe, McBath, Cruze and Monday. In Chief Reeder's group were Lieut. Phillips, Patrolmen Mynatt, McCrosskey, Constable Suffridge, Bob White, Jas. McIntosh and T. L. Reeder—a total of eighteen men. All of the officers and men were armed with Winchester rifles and had plenty of ammunition.[119]

Sheriff Walker met the Knoxville contingent at Trundle's Cross Road at midnight, and they arrived at the courthouse at 4:00 a.m. "Soon after the sheriff lodged in his own jail many men took their places around the jail and were made a guard by Deputy Davis and this morning one hundred armed men are guarding the jail."[120]

Toward sunrise crowds begin to gather in the town square, with people on both sides of the White Cap issue abandoning their farm work to stand eyeball-to-eyeball with their opposites. The tense standoff—White Caps facing both their angry neighbors and a formidable police presence—lasted hour after hour. But the standoff faded with the day, violence averted by law enforcement's show of force.

One final surreal scene during the trial for the murder of Bill Whaley emerged as the defense counsel was giving his final argument to the jury, and pleading for the acquittal of Wynn and Tipton, in the crowded and heavily guarded courtroom. With all the eloquence he could muster, while claiming that Pleas Wynn was an innocent man, the funeral cortege bearing the body of Wynn's brother, William, rolled slowly past the open window providing an eerie backdrop for the speech.

The jury got the case on the afternoon of April 8, 1898, and returned with its verdict the next day—Wynn and Tipton were both found guilty of first degree murder. Their capital murder case was appealed to the Tennessee Supreme Court, and the appeal was rejected on November 18, 1898. Their sentence—hanging by the neck until they were dead—was scheduled for January 4 1899.

Sheriff Maples was indicted for the killing of William Wynn, despite his claim that it was a case of self-defense.

---

[119] KILLED AT SEVIERVILLE, *The Knoxville Sentinel*, April 7, 1898
[120] Ibid

The latter part of the year also brought two other significant events to Sevier County.

First, Sheriff Maples, indicted and awaiting trial in the shooting death of William Wynn, was now dealing with the criminal justice system from the other side of the courtroom, pretty much removing any possibility of his re-election.

As previously stated, in 1898 there were about 4,000 registered voters in Sevier County, all men and comprising about a fifth of the county's population. More than 90 percent of the voters were reliably Republican. The county, like most of East Tennessee, swam against the political stream during the 1800s, opposing secession and staunchly supporting Republican candidates in every election that followed the Civil War.

Tom Davis was a lifelong Democrat, making him an outlier and someone probably accustomed to casting his vote for candidates whose chances of winning, if there were a Democrat on the ballot at all, were next to nil. But in the late summer of 1898 a lot of things were changing in Sevier County. One of them was that this Democrat, well-educated and respected even by those with whom he did not share a political philosophy, was recruited to run for High Sheriff. His relentless and courageous pursuit of Sevier County's White Caps put a sheen on his reputation that even his political affiliation could not obscure.

Davis's opponents that year were Republicans John Marshal and R. H. Shields, who was also respected as a man of honesty and character who believed in lawfulness, and was never suspected of supporting the White Caps. He was, however, also seen as not being as aggressive as Davis. He was rather quiet and unassuming, and content to leave the White Caps alone if they left him alone.

Sevier County had never before elected a Democratic sheriff, but in August the voters rewarded Thomas Houston Davis with that office for one two-year term beginning that year.

181

Of those roughly 4,000 registered voters, 3,529 cast their votes, and Davis won by a margin of 69 votes. In truth, the fight against the White Caps was behind him at that point, but the election did mean he would preside over the definitive event that could be considered the back breaker for the Grave Yard Hosts—the public executions of Tipton and Wynn.

As previously mentioned, the Law and Order League had formed as a coalition of law enforcement, jurists and lawyers in their attempt to decisively engage and defeat Whitecapism in Sevier County.

Cummings suggests members of that coalition were perfectly willing and able, just as the Blue Bills had been, to fight the White Caps in a way that perhaps was the only way they understood:

> Members of the law and order league were also not above using physical coercion to protect their candidate, and several of Davis's supporters waylaid and assaulted R. H. Shields, Davis's rival, on election day after accusing him of being a whitecap.[121]

A POLITICAL CARVING.

Defeated Knox County Candidate Seriously Stabbed.

KNOXVILLE, Tenn., Aug. 6.—(Special.) —R. H. Shields, the defeated Republican candidate for sheriff in Sevier county, was probably fatally stabbed today by W. H. Greer, a prominent Sevier county man.

The men quarreled over the result of the election, and later over the accusation alleged to have been made by Greer that Shields rented a house to a Whitecap. The affair has created considerable feeling in Sevier county.

---

[121] Cummings, 89

TOM DAVIS GETS THERE.

Elected Sheriff of Sevier County by Sixty-Nine Majority.

Special to The Sentinel.

Sevierville, Tenn., Aug. 5.—Thomas H. Davis, the well known deputy sheriff of Sevier county, has been elected sheriff of Sevier county. He is a democrat and in a county usually casting 4,000 votes, of which 400 or 500 are democratic. He received 1,799 votes and was elected with 69 majority.

This change is due to the fact that Mr. Davis has been the leader of the element which has demanded that law and order shall be supreme. He has done more than any other man to stop the reign of the white caps in that county and the establishment of law and order. His election is an endorsement of the man for his honesty of purpose and the defeat of the white cap element as well as the vote of the people to sustain Judge Nelson as judge of the circuit court and its officer. All of East Tennessee and in fact all parts of the state was interested in seeing Mr. Davis elected.

The total vote of the county is as follows:

SHERIFF.
T. H. Davis, dem 1,799
R. H. Shields, rep 1,730

Davis' majority 69
COUNTY COURT CLERK.
John Chandler, rep 2,857
J. J. Elerp, dem 537

Chandler's majority 2,320
CIRCUIT COURT CLERK.
R. P. Fowler, rep 2,568
A. C. Abbhley, dem 770

Fowler's majority 1,798
TRUSTEE.
W. C. Allen, rep 2,330
W. M. Mahan, dem 997

Allen's majority 1,353
Two districts unreported.
REGISTER.
Mac Murfee, rep 1,251
F. M. Williams, rep 1,543
W. C. Compton, rep 719

Williams' apparent plurality.... 292
Two districts yet to hear from.
In the Twenty-fifth district there was a fight growing out of the election in which R. H. Shields, the republican candidate for sheriff, was cut by W. H. Greer and it is thought that the injuries are serious.

There is considerable wild talk over the election of Davis as sheriff which will probably cool off after a few days.

The other momentous event scheduled that fall was the trying of the *State of Tennessee v. William Robert Catlett* on a charge of accessory before the fact of first degree murder in the death of Bill Whaley. Prosecutors may have sought to try Catlett in Bill Whaley's death first, because that was the case in which they had gotten conviction on both Pleas Wynn and J. C. Tipton.

The trial was scheduled for November, the same month in which the convictions of Wynn and Tipton were affirmed by the state's highest court.

By the final weeks of 1898, there was little doubt in most Sevier County minds that Bob Catlett was the driving force behind the murders of Bill and Laura Whaley, a belief reinforced by the convictions of Wynn and Tipton. Catlett, despite all his resources and family's social status , had become a pariah. The public's scorn ran deep and wide, and if assembling a reasonably objective jury for Wynn and Tipton had been difficult, it would be nearly impossible for Catlett.

Catlett's attorneys asked Judge Nelson for a change of venue to Hamblen County, a smaller county northeast of Sevier and separated by Jefferson County in between. Nelson granted the motion to move the trial, and it was rescheduled for December 1898 in Morristown.

The word was out by now that both Wynn and Tipton, having accepted the brevity of their futures, were ready to make soul-cleansing confessions about the Whaley killings, which could be key to the prosecution of Catlett. The state appealed to outgoing Governor Robert Taylor for a delay in the executions of the killers, which the governor granted, but not before the highly publicized and sensationalized drama of would the killers confess or would they not confess.

It was reported on December 7, 1898, less than a month before their scheduled executions, that Catlett Tipton had made a confession to Sheriff Fox.[122] It was reported a few days later that Pleas Wynn had also made a confession, and that they substantially corroborated each other, which is not surprising since they'd shared a Knox County jail cell for many months.

The state announced its readiness to go to trial at that point, but defense lawyers asked for a delay, saying they could not prepare an adequate case in just 30 days. Of course the defense, like everyone else involved, knew that by then Wynn and Tipton would have met their fate at the hand of the hangman, thus preventing two potential witnesses from testifying for the prosecution. Catlett's legal team wanted the trial reset to April 1899 during the next regular term of the Hamblen court.

The new judge in the case had a familiar face; Circuit Judge W. R. Hicks, whose lack of zealousness in rooting out and prosecuting White Caps had cost him his seat on the criminal court bench in Sevier County,

---

[122] IN WHALEY MURDER, *The Journal and Tribune*, December 7, 1898

would preside over the trial. But Hicks, possibly realizing the threat to his reputation and legacy, called a special term of the court in Hamblen to hear the Catlett case beginning February 6, 1899.

William R. "Bob" Catlett Trial I
February 1899

When the Catlett case was called in Morristown in February, the defense again begged for a delay, claiming that some of its witnesses could not be present and that it could not go to trial without them. Catlett was represented by W. J. McSween, George L. Zirkle, W. M. Mullendore and W. S. Dixon of Morristown.

But Hicks overruled the motion and straightway began empaneling a jury. Prosecutors G. M. Henderson, J. R. Penland, John B. Holloway of Morristown, and J. C. J. Williams of Knoxville opened the state's case the next morning.

The first witness, Lizzie Chandler, horrified Hamblen County jurors with the story of the night of the murders. The story of the wordless, merciless murders—which the woman had recounted with consistency through two trials already—transfixed the Hamblen courtroom. She once again identified Wynn as being one of the intruders, and testified that Tipton resembled the other in stature.

A couple more witnesses took the stand and were dismissed before the killers themselves were brought into the courtroom.

Wynn's detailed testimony only bolstered that of Lizzie Chandler, as he described how he and Tipton had met in Sevierville the night of the murders, how Tipton had retrieved his shotgun from a tool chest, how they had crossed the river and made their way to the Whaley cabin on foot, how while hiding outside that a noise they made had brought John Whaley to the door to investigate and how, after John Whaley had left, he and Tipton donned their White Cap masks and broke open the cabin door.

Wynn quoted the victims' pleadings and told how Tipton had fired the fatal shots, dropping the Whaleys together on the floor. And he described their retreat to Sevierville. Wynn said he had known Bob Catlett all his life and had seen him the morning of the murders at a stable in town. After helping Catlett get ready for his horse-trading trip to North Carolina, Wynn said, Catlett called him into a side room and asked if he had talked to J. C. Tipton about accompanying Tipton on the murder mission. Wynn testified he told Catlett he had, and Catlett then told him of the financial terms of the murder-for-hire.

Catlett said he wanted it done that night after he had left town.

Later, Wynn said, he and Tipton had met with James Catlett, Bob's brother, who told them that Bob Catlett had left $50 with him to be delivered to the killers after the job was done. Wynn said he collected his half of the blood money, $25, from James Catlett two days after the murders.

Confession of Pleas Wynn

"I know when the Whaleys were killed in Sevier County in December 1896. I was living in Sevierville, some two miles from the Whaley House. About dark on the night of the killing, Catlett Tipton and I met by agreement at Ben Bailey's house in Sevierville. From there we went to Bailey's shop, where Tipton worked. There Tipton got his shot gun out of a tool chest and he and I went down the west fork of Pigeon River to the junction of the two rivers. There we crossed the bridge over the east fork of the river and down the north side of the river, along the bank, till we got even with the Whaley house. We went up the hollow to within about twenty yards of the house, and then hearing some parties talking in the house we stopped, and after waiting a short time one of us coughed or made a noise. Immediately John Whaley, brother of William Whaley, came out with a pine torch and went to the crib nearby and did some nailing about the door, went back to the house, and in a few minutes left and went down the hollow toward where he lived, a few hundred yards away. Then Tipton and I masked ourselves and went to the door of William Whaley's house, broke it open and entered.

"William Whaley and wife were in the first bed on the right as we entered, and someone else I do not know was in another bed. William Whaley jumped out of bed and said:

'Have you come to kill us? Do anything else you want to us, but don't kill us.'

"Laura Whaley got out of bed and had her baby in her arms and went over toward the other bed, saying she wanted to give her baby to her sister. She gave it to some one who covered up her head.

"About this time Catlett Tipton shot William Whaley, who fell on the floor, and in another moment he shot Laura Whaley, who had turned to where her husband was standing when shot. She fell near him on the floor. Neither of the parties spoke after they were shot. Tipton had a double barrel shot gun, No. 12, and I had a No. 44 Smith & Wesson pistol. I did not fire a shot. We turned and walked out of the house without having spoken a word after we entered it.

"We next went directly back to Sevierville, crossing the ridges by a path leading east of Capt. Wynn's and into the road near J. W. Andes. At the lower end of Sevierville, at the bridge, Tipton and I separated, he going to Bailey's shop, as he said, and I going to O. L. Montgomery's in the upper end of town. I asked Montgomery if he was going fishing with us and he said no, that he was sick and could not go. I also asked the time of the night and ascertained that it was nearly nine o'clock.

"I went back in town and met Tipton on the old court house square near the Mitchell corner. From there we went to Mark McCowan's, a half mile below town, called him out and asked him to go fishing with us. He and his family were sick and he could not go. We got his canoe and went down the river a short distance below his house and cast two dynamites into the river and caught six fish—five suckers and one salmon. I took the suckers and Tipton the salmon and we returned to Sevierville. The town clock struck nine while we were talking to McCowan and ten just before we got back to town after the fishing. I stayed at home the rest of the night.

"I was well acquainted with the situation about the Whaley house. It was on my father's farm, and I had lived in the house about two years myself. I knew William Whaley tolerably well, and I knew his wife when I saw her. I never had any trouble with either of them nor ill will against them. Neither of them ever did me any harm, so far as I know.

"I know the defendant, Bob Catlett. Have known him nearly all my life. I saw him on the morning before the Whaleys were killed. He came into Sevierville with some horses and went to Lovedays stable and put them up. I met him in the street and went to the stable with him. From there we went to M. R. Rawling's saddle shop, where I helped Catlett fix his saddle girth. We were there some little time. No one was with us. We then went to Fred Emert's store, then to Trotter's hardware store, next to John Yett's store, and finally to West Emert's store, trying to buy a certain kind of whip Catlett wanted. I went to W. R. Montgomery's office and tried to get one from him, as he had what Catlett wanted.

188

"We then returned to Loveday's stable, where Catlett's horses were. While there, Catlett took me back into the stable in a side room, and there he mentioned to me the first time about putting the Whaleys out of the way. He asked me if I had had a talk with Catlett Tipton lately, and if I had agreed to go to a certain place with him. I told him I had talked with him and I had agreed to go. He told me he had agreed to pay Tipton fifty dollars to kill the Whaleys, pay his lawyers' fees and keep him out of jail if anything should be found out on him. He said that Whaley and his wife were witnesses against him and he wanted them killed so they could not testify against him, and he wanted it done that night, while he was away, so he would not be suspected and could prove where he was. He left Sevierville with four horses, about twelve o'clock, I think, saying he was going to Rolen's that night.

"I saw J. M. Catlett, brother of Bob Catlett, that same evening. He, Tipton and myself had a talk at a blacksmith shop near the old jail place that evening. No one else was present. Catlett said that Bob had left fifty dollars with him to be paid when the Whaleys were put out of the way. Jim Catlett was drinking that evening. The second day after the killing, as I now remember, Tipton paid me twenty-five dollars. This is all that I ever got for the part I took in that murder.

"I was arrested, tried and convicted with Tipton for the killing of the Whaleys. We appealed our case to the supreme court and there it was affirmed."

On cross examination, defense attorneys grilled Wynn about his own trial, at which he had denied any involvement in the murders. But Wynn acknowledged that that testimony was false and designed only to obtain an acquittal on the charges for himself. He testified that at the end of

December 1898, at the urging of his wife and a minister of the gospel, he had decided to give a true account of the killings to the court. The testimony, he said, was given without any promise of leniency for him and in the full knowledge that his execution would proceed on schedule.

Tipton joined his cohort in confessing his role in the killings and the complicity of Bob Catlett. Tipton told of the repeated attempts by Catlett to get him to kill the Whaleys so that they could not implicate Catlett in the rock-and-buckshot assault on the Walter Maples home. Tipton detailed the events leading up to him agreeing to commit the murders, and Catlett promising to take care of any bond or legal fees that should arise.

Tipton's account of the day of the murders aligned with Wynn's, and he acknowledged that he was the one who shot both Whaleys in the head. He told of returning to town and going dynamite fishing with Wynn later that night. He said James Catlett had come to Sevierville the next day and paid him the $50 for the killings and that he had given half of it to Wynn.

He also said he never harbored any animosity toward either Bill or Laura Whaley.

Confession of J. Catlett Tipton

"I was born and raised in Sevier County; I am about 38 years old. In December, 1896, I was living about two miles from Sevierville, but was at that time staying with Ben Bailey, my brother-in-law, and working in the blacksmith shop with him. I know the defendant, Bob Catlett and have known him pretty much my whole life.

"On the Saturday evening that the November term of the court adjourned, Bob Catlett came to me and said he wanted to have a talk with me. We went into Fred Emert's store and upstairs and into a back room. He there told me that William Whaley and wife had gone before the grand jury at that term of court and had indicted him and Bob Wade, his brother-in-law, for shooting into Walter Maples' house. He said he wanted them put out of the way and would give one hundred dollars to kill them, that he wanted to make an example of them to teach people that they could not swear against him. I told him I did not want to do it and would not do it. This was about all that occurred there, and we went out of the store. Bob Wade was present during this conversation.

"There was a meeting of an Odd Fellows lodge that night at Pigeon Forge, about eight miles above Sevierville. Wm. Wynn, Jesse Atchley and I went to it, leaving Sevierville that evening. I went in a buggy with Wm. Wynn, I think. Some time after the lodge had been in session, Bob Catlett and Bob Wade came in. That is the first time I ever knew Catlett or Wade in that lodge and have never seen them there since. It was about fourteen miles from there to where Catlett lived. As we were returning from the lodge that night, I stopped on the road near Henderson's Island at a turnip patch and got some turnips and distributed them among the crowd.

"There were several among, including Bob Catlett, Bob Wade, Arthur Seaton, Schuyler Atchley, Jesse Atchley and Wm. Wynn. Wade and Catlett were riding horse-back, and when ready to leave the turnip patch, Bob Catlett suggested to Wade that he take my seat in the buggy and for me to get on Wade's horse, as he wanted to talk with me. This change was accordingly made and I rode from there to Rambo's lane, about three miles, with Bob Catlett.

"On this trip he again brought up the subject of the Whaleys and renewed his proposition to me to put them out of the way for him. I told him I did not want to do it, but before leaving me near the Rambo lane, he handed me an envelope and said for me to take it and that it was mine when the Whaleys were put out of the way.

"I took the package and went on home from that point. I examined the contents of the envelope and found it consisted of four twenty dollar bills and one twenty dollar gold piece. I kept the money until the next Wednesday evening, and then I took it to Yett's store in Sevierville and gave it to J. R. Yett and told him to put it in his safe for me for a short time. I let it stay there until Friday following, when I got it and gave it back to Bob Catlett, saying to him at the time that I had decided not to do the job and returned his money. Catlett replied that he was glad of it for he could get it done for one-half of that amount.

"It was not long, however, until Catlett returned to me again and began to beg me to comply with his wishes by putting the Whaleys out of the way. I guess, in all, he must have come to me some twelve or fifteen different times, and I at last consented to kill the Whaleys for him, for which he agreed to pay me fifty dollars, and, if I got into any trouble over it, he was to pay my attorney's fees and keep me out of jail by making bond for me. On one occasion I told Catlett I had spoken to Pleas Wynn to go with me and that he had agreed to go. He asked me if I thought Pleas would be all right and I told him I did. It was agreed that Catlett should go south with some stock and that the Whaleys should be killed while he was gone, in order that he might not be suspicioned.

"Catlett went through Sevierville on Monday morning, the 28th of December 1896, with some horses, and as he was going out of Sevierville, near the Southern Methodist Church, I met him and helped him straighten out one of his horses. While there he said to me:

"Be certain and attend to that job tonight."

192

"Jim Catlett, a brother of Bob, told me that evening that Bob had left the money with him to pay for killing the Whaleys, whenever the work was done, and that he (Jim) would pay the money. This talk was had in the presence of Pleas Wynn near the old jail place in Sevierville.

"That night, the 28th of December 1896, Pleas Wynn and I by agreement met at Ben Bailey's, in Sevierville, and about dark we left there, going first to Bailey's shop near the bank of the west fork of the Pigeon river. There I got my shot gun out of my tool chest, together with some cartridges. Leaving the shop, we went down the bank of said river to the point or junction of the two rivers, and crossing the bridge over the east fork of the river we proceeded down the bank of said river on the north side to the Capt. Wynn farm . When we got even with the Whaley house, we left the river and went up the hollow to where the Whaleys lived . We stopped a short distance from the house. We saw a light in the house and heard some one talking within. Wynn, as I now remember, made a noise by coughing and a man who I suppose was John Whaley came out with a light and did some fixing about the crib door. He returned to the house, and in a short time left.

"Wynn and I then masked ourselves heavily and proceeded to the house, where the door was bursted open and we entered the house. I had my shot gun and Wynn had a pistol. I there killed both Whaley and his wife by shooting them in the head. I never spoke to anyone after I entered the house, nor did either William or Laura Whaley speak after they were shot, to my knowledge. I reloaded my gun and then Wynn and I returned to Sevierville.

"We did not return as we went, but took a nearer route across the ridges, coming into the road near where the Andes boys live , just below Sevierville. I took my gun back to the shop and put it in the tool chest and got some dynamite I had there and met Pleas Wynn near the Mitchell corner in town. He said he had been to Otis Montgomery's.

"From there we went to Mark McCowan's, a half mile below town, called him out, talked to him awhile and asked him to go fishing with us, but he declined , saying his folks were sick. We got his canoe and went down the river a short distance and dropped two sticks of dynamite in the river. The result was we got six fish - one salmon and five suckers. We took the canoe back to the bank and left it where McCowan told us to. Before leaving the canoe we there burned our masks. We then went on to Sevierville, where we divided the fish , he taking the five suckers and I the salmon. I went to Ben Bailey's, where I boarded , and went to bed, and I suppose Wynn went home.

"I was barely acquainted with Wm. Whaley; knew him when I saw him. I never saw Laura Whaley until the night she was killed . I never had had any trouble with either one of them, and had no ill will or malice toward them. "Jim Catlett came to Sevierville the next day after the Whaleys were killed and paid me the fifty dollars, according to agreement, and on the following day (I think it was) I gave Pleas Wynn half of it.

"When I gave the package of money to J. R. Yett to deposit in his safe for me, Wm. Marshall and Miller Yett were present, and when I took it away George Nichols and one or two others were present. I never deposited money or anything else with J. R. Yett & Co. at any other time, to my recollection."

Tipton's cross examination mirrored Wynn's, including an admission that the testimony of innocence in his earlier trial had been untrue.

' I am now and have been for a good while confined in the Knoxville jail . I swore some three or four times when on trial myself that I did not kill the Whaleys and that I did not know who did; that if Bob Catlett had anything to do with it I did not know it . But that was false; I swore it to save my life and to get out of my trouble, if I could. I have not been promised anything nor given to understand that my sentence would be commuted if I would make a statement implicating Bob Catlett in the murder of the Whaleys. I was advised by my friends that if I knew anything about the Whaley murder I ought to tell it, and I decided a short time ago that I would tell the whole story as I knew it , and this I have done on the witness stand today. It is the truth."

James Catlett testified after Tipton, adamantly denying that he had any role in the murders or that he had paid Tipton any money following the killings. Bob Wade also denied from the witness stand that he had any involvement, and the defense rested.

In rebuttal, prosecutors elicited testimony from an assistant cashier at the Bank of Sevierville named A. T. Marshall. Marshall testified that James Catlett had withdrawn $50 from the bank on the day after the Whaleys were killed, and produced bank books that reflected that transaction.

After five days of testimony, Judge Hicks charged the jury on Friday evening, February 10, 1899.

After all that testimony the jury was unable to reach a verdict, and Judge Hicks called a mistrial and set a new trial for the regular court term beginning April 24, 1899. The case against Bob Wade was nolle prossed on March 21, 1899, meaning prosecutors had decided not to pursue the charges against him. The next day, James M. Catlett, Bob's brother, was indicted as an accessory before the fact in the murder of William Whaley.

195

Davis was quoted in a Knoxville newspaper as saying the jurors had been bribed or coerced, but there were only four jurors who were for conviction: "R. L. Love, J. L. McGhee, John L. Williams and James Noe. For acquittal were J. H Turner, William Treece, John Noe, James Williams, Fred Jones, Julian Hacker, Levi Ivy, and Levi Bruce."[123]

It is worth mentioning Montgomery once again cast doubt upon his Whitecap affiliation by agreeing with Sheriff Davis. Montgomery said, "It looks like the man of wealth and influence who incited the hellish deed killing the Whaleys will escape while the poor wretches who were duped into doing his dirty work will have to suffer."[124]

The rift between Montgomery and The Law and Order League had not gone away, and the editor of the Vindicator blamed the outside influence on Sheriff Davis, whom he considered "the linchpin of foreign influence in Sevier County."[125] Montgomery was also critical of the time Davis spent away from his county, presumably working on improving relations with his allies in Knox County. He was lying in wait for the opportunity to continue his attack on Sheriff Davis, and when the opportunity presented itself he took full aim at Davis.

Between the trials Sheriff Davis stated in a newspaper article that he believed they would secure a conviction against Bob Catlett in the second trial: "You know Catlett Tipton was acquitted, when he was tried for murdering the man; but we got him on the second trial for murdering the woman. I firmly believe we will convict Bob Catlett of hiring this deed done, when we arraign on this second charge."[126]

William R. "Bob" Catlett Trial II
May 22, 1899

---

[123] CATLETT CASE A MISTRIAL, The Weekly Sentinel, February 15, 1899
[124] A MISTRIAL, *Vindicator*, February 15, 1899
[125] Cummings, 93
[126] MAY CONVICT BOB CATLETT, , May 24, 1899

The new Tennessee governor, Benton McMillin, was asked for another 90-day delay in the executions of Pleas Wynn and J. C. Tipton. He agreed, and in May 1899 the two convicted murderers were set to testify a second time against Bob Catlett in Morristown in the death of Bill Whaley.

"On the first day of the trial, however, Attorney General Henderson announced that he did not believe the state had sufficient evidence to convict the defendant and asked for a delay. Judge Hicks rejected the state's request and in a surprise move dismissed the charges against Catlett. Before a new warrant could be served upon Catlett, he escaped."[127]

One newspaper reported it differently, reporting that "Attorney-General G. Henderson addressed the court, stating several of the state's witnesses were unable to be present, on account of sickness. He suggested that the case be nolle prossed. This was done, and Catlett was liberated and is a free man."[128]

The reason it is worth pointing out the differences in the two reports is subtle, but necessary. The quote from the Cummings thesis states that Judge Hicks' dismissal was a "surprise move," but that's not the case because Attorney General Henderson made a motion that the case be nolle prossed—which is in effect a motion to dismiss. That being said, it should not have been a surprise since the motion was made.

The circumstances of the inability of Sheriff Davis to arrest Catlett are murky at best, and there was plenty of finger pointing by all involved. And as you might expect, the reports of Catlett's "escape" varied from source to source, and Montgomery relished in the opportunity to hang the responsibility squarely on Davis.

---

[127] Cummings, 93
[128] BOB CATLETT A FREE MAN, *Knoxville Sentinel*, May 22, 1899+

Montgomery excoriated Davis in the days and weeks following Catlett's escape, and even postulated in the Vindicator that "there is a probability that a movement will be made at the July term of the county court to declare the office of sheriff vacant and elect a successor to Tom Davis, the present sheriff."[129]

Davis was more than able to defend his actions, and did so in the Knoxville Sentinel on June 6, 1899:[130]

"Montgomery is a white cap, and he runs a white cap paper. He has always been opposed to me, because I was opposed to the white caps, and brought them to justice. Montgomery says the county court may ask for my resignation, because I have spent too much time away from this place. I have been away in business, and I have done my duty as conscientiously as any sheriff could. I am not afraid of the county court seeking to impeach me, because I know the court is not made up of white caps."

The next day Montgomery even suggested that Catlett's escape was conspiratorial: "Is this the plan, and does this theory explain why Catlett was permitted to escape? An indignant people await an explanation."[131] On that same day Montgomery, in an editorial, made the observation: "Bob Catlett and Tom Davis have not yet made a collision, but it is not known whether Bob is evading Tom or Tom evading Bob."[132]

It was reported in the Knoxville Sentinel that Attorney General Henderson wrote a letter to a "gentleman in this city" on the heels of the

[129] MAY REMOVE SHERIFF DAVIS, *Knoxville Sentinel*, May 26, 1899
[130] DAVIS AND CATLETT IN SEVIER COUNTY, *Knoxville Sentinel*, June 6, 1899
[131] "Law and Order.", *The Vindicator*, June 7, 1899
[132] W. R. Montgomery, *The Vindicator*, June 7, 1899

ongoing rift between Sheriff Davis and the Editor of the Vindicator.[133]
The following is reportedly an excerpt from Henderson's letter:

"I am much surprised that Davis has allowed Catlett to escape, and has failed to carry out his part of the program. I told Davis, in the court house in Morristown, when the case was dismissed, that he ought to arrest Catlett before he left Morristown. I told him to keep Catlett under the closest surveillance, and not let him escape. I only agreed to the nolle prosse course taken after I was advised to take it by Mr. Penland and Sheriff Davis, and I stated to them I had some serious misgivings as to the result of the course agreed upon. Davis may get Catlett back in due time. If not, I leave the responsibility where it belongs."

It was clearly in Catlett's best interest to remain in hiding until the executions of Tipton and Wynn were carried out, and with Catlett missing "Governor Benton McMillan announced there would be no more reprieves for Tipton and Wynn."[134] They were set to be hanged by their necks until declared dead on July 5, 1899.

Bob Catlett stayed "on the run" until he negotiated his surrender in November 1901.

---

[133] BLAMES SHERIFF DAVIS, *Knoxville Sentinel*, June 14, 1899
[134] Cummings, 94

24

Last Steps

The ropes that would dispatch Pleas Wynn and J. C. Tipton into the hereafter had been stretching for months at the Knox County Jail, where the two convicted killer were housed. An unstretched rope can make for a very messy hanging, and since this was to be the first execution in Sevier County in 90 years, officials wanted the hanging to go as well as possible.

The Knoxville Sentinel reported on July 3, 1899, that Sheriff Davis "and a force of regular and special deputies, arrived in the city this morning, to convey to Sevierville the two condemned men, Pleas Wynn and Catlett Tipton."[135]

When Wynn learned the sheriff had an escort of fifteen deputies he smiled, and went on to say there wouldn't be any trouble on their way back to Sevierville. Wynn also said he wished Sheriff Davis would hang him, and that he considered Davis neither a friend nor an enemy.

It was reported in the same article that "Sheriff Fox took Wynn to the photograph gallery this morning, when he and his wife were

---

[135] Sheriff Davis and Posse Have Arrived, *Knoxville Sentinel*, July 3, 1899

photographed together. The sheriff then took them to Peter Kern's, where they ate ice cream."

Wynn and Tipton asked that The Sentinel print the following card of thanks:

"We want to say through the columns of The Sentinel, a word in behalf of Sheriff J. W. Fox and his jailers, Tom Bell and Lee. Since we have been in the Knox County jail these men have treated us very kindly, and we fully appreciate the treatment of us. Sheriff Fox knows how to gain the confidence of the prisoners, and they soon learn to respect him. We wish to thank him publicly for the treatment of ourselves and relatives who have called to see us.

"We wish also to return our thanks to the ladies and ministers, who have regularly called at the jail, and especially Mrs. J. R. Lauritzen, Mrs. Skillman and Miss Kinzel, all of whom have called at the jail every Sunday, with one or two exceptions, since we have been here. Other friends have also been kind to us, for which we are grateful.

"PLEAS WYNN,
"CATLETT TIPTON."

The next day, Independence Day, 1899, Wynn and Tipton arose early and prepared for their final ride to the Sevier County Courthouse. Their 20-mile journey in a four-seat hack began at 7:15 in the morning. Accompanying the carriage was an escort of 15 deputized men, including Sevier County High Sheriff Tom Davis and Knox County Sheriff J. W. Fox, who provided the ropes, tied the nooses and had black hoods made for the condemned.

Along the route, the entourage made several stops so Wynn and Tipton could say final goodbyes to friends and acquaintances. They even received ovations at Catlettsburg and Boyds Creek., but there were no attempts to free the men.

The troupe arrived at Sevierville at 12:45 p.m., and the convicted killers ate a meal prepared for them at 1:00 at the jail.

Crowds of people began gathering in town the day before the noon hangings—thousands of them.

A Knoxville Sentinel headline on the day of the executions, July 5, 1899, proclaimed, "Stroke of twelve sounds death knell."

A special breakfast was prepared for the men on the morning of their execution, July 5, 1899, and was served in the corridors of the jail. Sheriff Fox provided Wynn a razor so that he would not have to meet his Maker with a stubble. Wynn also shaved Tipton.

People gathered in small groups outside the execution enclosure, talking in hushed tones. Anticipation began to rise as noon approached, but Sheriff Davis granted the men's request for a delay so that they could have one extra hour with their families.

It's not clear when Pleas Wynn asked to be baptized and the request granted, but it did happen. At that time the Little Pigeon River ran within a few dozen yards of the Sevier County courthouse, and Pleas Wynn repented, at least outwardly. Only he and God knew what was truly in his heart, but Wynn requested he be allowed to have a clergyman baptize him before his death, which was granted.

In front of a primitive camera on the far side of the river, Wynn, a minister and another man who resembles a pen-and-ink portrait of Tom Davis waded into the water in front of hundreds of observers on the riverbank and on the roof of the jail. Wynn was immersed and drawn forth from the water, trusting his profession of faith was acceptable in the eyes of God.

Tipton's relationship with God is less clear. He did not join Wynn in baptism that day, possibly because he had already undergone that ritual.

Or maybe he simply had not been touched by a providential hand as his co-defendant apparently had.

Hundreds of onlookers line the riverbank and perch on the roof of the jail as Pleas Wynn, convicted in the murders of Bill and Laura Whaley, prepares to be baptized in the Little Pigeon River. Less than an hour later Wynn was hanged on the courthouse lawn.

–Photo courtesy of Carroll McMahan

At some point after the extra hour was granted Sheriff Davis read the death warrants.

At 12;45 Sheriff Davis, who was on the outside of the jail, told Deputies Keener and Nicely to bring the prisoners out, and the walk to the scaffold commenced, the condemned surrounded by deputies and led by Davis.

A newspaper dispatch—proudly announcing it was delivered "by long-distance telephone" from Sevierville to the Knoxville Journal and Tribune—said the town was eerily quiet in the overcast July humidity as Wynn and Tipton took their final steps up to the gallows platform. They were asked if they had anything else to say, but both indicated their final statements had been written beforehand.

Tipton had admonished, "Tell the young men to keep good company. Bad company has brought me to this." Likewise, Wynn wrote, "Tell the boys to be obedient to their parents."

On the gallows, Wynn and Tipton said their final farewells to their families with kisses and had a last word with clergy, and they sang a verse of the hymn "I Need Thee Every Hour." The ministers offered a final prayer for the men's souls just before the hoods were placed on their heads. John S. Springs, the postmaster for Emert's Cove, who had vocally and publicly chastised the White Caps over their killing of Eli Williamson, placed the nooses around the condemned men's necks and tightened them up.

Published reports said the two seemed resigned to their fate and calm in their demeanor as the moment of their deaths approached. Four physicians were recruited to certify the expiration of the condemned.

Once on the platform, Davis was more or less an observer, with only one more action to take. He looked up from the platform deck to his deputy, J. E. Keener, who was standing at the opposite corner with his hand on the release lever, and gave him a silent and almost imperceptible nod.

It was 1:02 in the afternoon of July 5, 1899.

Davis probably did not even see the ugliest part of it from his perch on the gallows platform. With a clunking sound as the trapdoors beneath them swung open, Wynn and Tipton dropped six feet down, as far as the ropes would allow. Wynn jerked and quivered and audibly strangled before being pronounced dead 13 minutes later. Tipton's neck was broken, but the rope also opened up his throat from one jaw to the other. Blood poured from the wound down the front of his clothing. He was certified dead 18 minutes after he dropped through the trapdoor..

The Journal and Tribune headline in Knoxville, Tennessee read "BLOOD WILL HAVE BLOOD" on July 6, 1899.

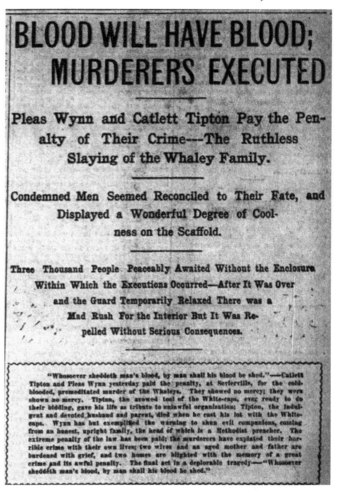

BLOOD WILL HAVE BLOOD; MURDERERS EXECUTED

Pleas Wynn and Catlett Tipton Pay the Penalty of Their Crime---The Ruthless Slaying of the Whaley Family.

Condemned Men Seemed Reconciled to Their Fate, and Displayed a Wonderful Degree of Coolness on the Scaffold.

Three Thousand People Peaceably Awaited Without the Enclosure Within Which the Executions Occurred—After It Was Over and the Guard Temporarily Relaxed There was a Mad Rush For the Interior But It Was Repelled Without Serious Consequences.

"Whosoever sheddeth man's blood, by man shall his blood be shed."—Catlett Tipton and Pleas Wynn yesterday paid the penalty, at Sevierville, for the cold-blooded, premeditated murder of the Whaleys. They showed no mercy; they were shown no mercy. Tipton, the avowed tool of the White-caps, ever ready to do their bidding, gave his life as tribute to unlawful organization; Tipton, the indulgent and devoted husband and parent, died when he cast his lot with the White-caps. Wynn has but exemplified the warning to shun evil companions, coming from an honest, upright family, the head of which is a Methodist preacher. The extreme penalty of the law has been paid; the murderers have explated their horrible crime with their own lives; two wives and an aged mother and father are burdened with grief, and two homes are blighted with the memory of a great crime and its awful penalty. The final act is a deplorable tragedy—"Whosoever sheddeth man's blood, by man shall his blood be shed."

The bodies of Wynn and Tipton were cut down from the scaffold and turned over to their families. Wynn was buried that afternoon in Shiloh Memorial Cemetery in Pigeon Forge. Tipton was buried the next morning at 9 o'clock in Roberts Cemetery on Jayell Road.

William Robert "Bob" Catlett Trial III
February 1903

Bob Catlett's whereabouts from May 1899 to November 1901 are a mystery, other than one alleged sighting in Knoxville in October 1900. His brother, James M. Catlett, was tried as an accessory before the fact in the death of Bill Whaley in Sevier County in the early days of 1900, but on January 5 it ended in a mistrial. He asked for and was granted a change of venue to Blount County on May 16, 1900, and won an acquittal at trial.

It was reported in the 4 o'clock edition of the Knoxville Sentinel on Friday, November 8, 1901, that Bob Catlett had surrendered and made bond to Sheriff R. H. Shields, after being a fugitive from justice since May 1899.[136]

Tom Davis, then the former High Sheriff of Sevier County, addressed Catlett's situation in the Knoxville Sentinel on November 9, 1901. Davis speculated that Catlett had hiding in Georgia, South Carolina and Kentucky, but mostly in Sevier County.

It was February 10, 1903, before Bob Catlett faced another courtroom, charged with procuring the killing of William Whaley and wife, in Sevier County, some years ago."[137] By this time, the case against Catlett hinged not on the testimony of Pleas Wynn and J. C. Tipton, but on transcripts of it. As in his first trial, the Loudon County jury "stood ten for murder in the first degree and two for acquittal,"[138] and he once again obtained a mistrial.

William Robert "Bob" Catlett Trial IV
June 8-13, 1903

His retrial in her murder came June 8, 1903, and after five days of testimony, the jury returned a verdict of "Murder in the First Degree,"[139]

---

[136] CATLETT SURRENDERS; NOW OUT UNDER BOND, *Knoxville Sentinel*, November 8, 1901

[137] CATLETT ON TRIAL, *Knoxville Sentinel*, February 11, 1903

[138] CATLETT MISTRIAL, *Knoxville Sentinel*, February 18, 1903

[139] BOB CATLETT SENTENCED TO HANG AT SEVIERVILLE, FRIDAY, JULY 31, *Knoxville Sentinel*, June 13, 1903

and it was held by the judge that there were no mitigating circumstances in the case. Bob Catlett was at last convicted and sentenced to the same fate as Catlett Tipton and Pleas Wynn—he was sentenced to hanged at Sevierville, Friday, July 31, 1903.

But on October 31, 1903, the Tennessee Supreme Court reversed the conviction. The court ruled that even though the prior testimony of Wynn and Tipton was admissible by transcript, certain restrictions should have been placed on it, and a stenographer's notes should not have been read to the jury. There were also claims that some jurors who said they had heard of the case and had already formed opinions were seated over the objections of the defense. Together, the court said, that constituted reversible error and it sent the case back to the lower court.

William Robert "Bob" Catlett Trial V
April 4-9, 1904

Bob Catlett was tried again in a Loudon County courtroom beginning April 4, 1904. After a five-day trial with restrictions on the transcript testimony of Wynn and Tipton adhered to, on April 9, 1904, the Knoxville Weekly headline screamed: ROBERT CATLETT ACQUITTED IN THE WHALEY CASES.

The murder for hire saga of the Whaleys in Sevier County was over.

25

Thomas Houston Davis

Y ou might know Sevier County is the home of Dolly Parton and Dollywood, and probably Pigeon Forge and Gatlinburg, however, the Sevier County of the 1890s was more akin to the Wild West. But chances are if you're not from Sevier County, you probably had never heard of Tom Davis. And if you are from Sevier County, unless you know about the White Caps bloody reign of terror and their primary adversary, you probably had not heard of Tom Davis. There was a time, while he was in dogged pursuit of the White Caps, that his exploits were legendary. If there were an equivalent of Mount Rushmore for Tennessee Sheriffs, Thomas Houston Davis would occupy one of those places.

In many ways, Davis ran against the grain of the time and place in which he lived. He was born, August 7, 1864, and he died on August 1, 1930, just six days shy of his sixty-sixth birthday.

The son of J. D. Davis and the former Mary Pickens, daughter of Sevier County Judge G. Samuel Pickens, was born into a farm family that was flourishing in the heat of both a Tennessee summer and a fading Civil War.

The Davises saw to it that young Tom regularly attended public schools, before moving on to a couple of terms at Carson College in Jefferson County and then to Knoxville Business College.

By adulthood he had some portion of a college education behind him, which really gave him an advantage in his determination to eradicate Whitecapping from Sevier County. He was a Democrat in a county so Republican that election day was more or less a formality, but he won the confidence of Sevier Countians as an anti-Whitecap force.

Davis taught school briefly but eventually returned to the family farm. At age 23 he married Linnie Adams of Strawberry Plains, and from their wedding day in 1887 they settled into a quiet farm life for seven years.

For Tom Davis to choose to become a lawman seemed out of character, yet considering how deeply he abhorred the violence in his county and those responsible for it, perhaps it was a sense of community that led him to take the oath of a deputy in 1894. And perhaps it was genetic; his maternal grandfather had been a judge.

Whatever the reason, Davis became a worthy and determined nemesis of the White Caps, pursuing them near and far, and for weeks and months at a time. They knew that Davis's smiling face masked a determination to run them to ground, in the same way their hoods masked their identities and evil intent.

He framed the fight against the White Caps by saying that "the time has come when some man must undertake it, or our county is ruined." During the course of his several years in law enforcement, Tom Davis would arrest or assist in the arrest of 34 White Caps.

Thomas Houston Davis only served one two-year term as High Sheriff of Sevier County, leaving office in 1900 without running for re-election. When asked why he was not running for re-election, he stated his case:

"I was deputy sheriff for four years and my object in seeking the place of sheriff was to break up the lawlessness of the white caps, and I think I have aided in doing so. There are no longer any signs of their operations in the county. I will move to Knoxville when my present term expires, and may go into the livery business, although I hear it is crowded. There are four Republicans out for sheriff in Sevier so far, but I do not know whether the democrats will put out a man."[140]

He remains the first and last Democrat elected to that office. According to the Knoxville Sentinel edition on Tuesday, September 18, 1900, he purchased the livery business of Scott & Chanaberry at 113 Vine Avenue in Knoxville.[141]

Tom Davis the fiddle player? The Journal and Tribune reported on February 15, 1900, that Sheriff Tom Davis was a member of the Brotherhood of Fiddlers, whose members were giving a concert in Maryville in Columbian Hall.[142]

Evidently Tom Davis was by nature a law enforcement officer, as he served as a railway detective in St Louis during the World's Fair from 1902-1903.[143] He moved to Florida and served as a detective, then in 1911-1912 he was the chief of police in Jellico. He was chief of police in Etowah from 1920 to 1922, after he an unsuccessful run for Sheriff of Knox County in 1920, losing by only 164 votes. His campaign advertisements

---

[140] "Will Not Run Again", *The Journal and Tribune*, Knoxville, Tennessee, June 3, 1900

[141] NOW IN LIVERY BUSINESS, Knoxville Sentinel, September 18, 1900

[142] FIDDLERS GO TO MARYVILLE, *The Journal and Tribune*, Knoxville, Tennessee, February 15, 1900

[143] Yadon, Unmasking the Sevier County White-Caps, *The Knoxville News-Sentinel*, June 2, 1929

in the local papers centered around his campaign to end Whitecapping and lawlessness in Sevier County in the 1890s.

The final records of him list his occupation as "real estate" and his residence as Knoxville, specifically the Beverly Hills Sanatorium, where he was being treated for tuberculosis.

The sanatorium was opened in 1924 under the sponsorship of the Knoxville Civitan Club and was operated by the city. Davis's death certificate indicates he had been under treatment for tuberculosis for three years and that a contributing cause of death was "senility."

He died at 9:20 a.m. on August 1, 1930, at age 65 having achieved his goal of defeating the White Caps, but without seeing one of his prime targets, Bob Catlett, punished.

He is buried in Alder Branch Cemetery in Sevier County.

CLEANED OUT NOTORIOUS BAND

Tom Davis, Sheriff During Exciting White Cap Days In 90's, Dies Peacefully at Sanatorium.

TOM DAVIS
The man who cleaned up Sevier County in the White Cap days of more than 30 years ago, Tom Davis, former sheriff, died Friday after being an invalid a year.

EPILOGUE

The White Caps were not much of a factor in Sevier County by the early years of the 20th century, outside of some lingering suspicions and animosities that were more personal than organizational. The raids stopped, but the wariness between individuals over what may have been done to whom by whom hung on well into the 1950s or 60s.

Most anyone directly involved in White Cap or Blue Bill activity or even law enforcement or the court system was dead by then. But family ties being as strong as they are in rural, mountain communities, there were many who were only one generation removed who still did not want anyone talking bad about their ancestors, or still held another family responsible for a loss in their own.

That is one reason the story of the White Cap era has always been a dubious undertaking and never written down in any cohesive fashion, most of it not recorded at all.

The families involved—the Davises and the Hendersons, the Catletts, Tiptons and Wynns, and the McMahans and Whaleys—find their surnames on any number of streets and other landmarks in the 21st Century. But Sevier County, a dusty agricultural county in the 1890s, is now populated by bungee jumps, go-carts, goofy golf, zip lines, chain restaurants and hotels. The Great Smoky Mountains National Park, which now occupies a substantial swath of Sevier County, attracts as many as 10 million visitors a year, more than any other national park. Copeland Creek, where this all began, is now inside the national park.

There are still those who do not have much enthusiasm for any retelling of the White Cap-Blue Bill saga. But it is a part of Sevier County's history, and there is no pretending it did not happen even if some of the loose ends are never neatly tied off.

212

And so here is how the story ends: Every indication is that Bob Catlett got away with murder. There is almost nothing that would refute that, and there is ample evidence, circumstantial and testimonial, that he was materially and financially at the core of a conspiracy that brutally took the lives of a young couple, thus orphaning an infant girl named Molly. He was even convicted of it once, though that was overturned on a technicality.

Both Pleas Wynn and J. C. Tipton testified to Catlett's involvement, even though they had no reason to accuse him if he were not part of the plot and nothing to gain by fabricating it. They had already exhausted their appeals, and their confessions containing the accusations against Catlett were not going to prevent their appointment with a hangman. There was also the matter of the $50 bank withdrawal by Bob Catlett's brother, James, the day after the killings—the exact sum of money that Wynn and Tipton said they were paid for the act, the money delivered by James Catlett.

Bob Catlett outlived virtually everyone else in the White Cap saga. He died November 25, 1940, a resident of Knoxville, at age 84. Cas Walker attempted to get him to open up about it just three years before his death, but was given a stern warning not to ever open his gate again.

Bob Catlett is buried in the two-century-old Shiloh Memorial Cemetery in Pigeon Forge alongside his wife, Mary Ann. He outlived her, too. Also buried nearby is Bob Wade, Mary Ann's brother, who was not prosecuted in the Whaley murders.

There is a saying that admonishes people to keep their friends close and their enemies even closer. Some have said that Wade's prime concern through all of this was the safety and wellbeing of his sister. He knew of Catlett's volatile nature, and that by being shoulder-to-shoulder with him he could act as not only a shield for Mary Ann, but also as a force to mitigate some of Catlett's darker motivations. But obviously not all of them. This is questionable though, given that Catlett was sixteen years older than Wade.

It can also be speculated that Wade may have been something of an information source for the authorities, if not during the initial phases of the investigation of the murders, then possibly after his own culpability became manifest. That might explain the decision not to prosecute him as part of the conspiracy, even though, according to testimony, he was present at meetings where the murders were discussed before they were carried out, and he alerted no one.

Even without Wade, all the circumstances that immediately followed the Whaley murders and the rapid arrests of Wynn, Tipton, Catlett and Wade would indicate that someone with intimate knowledge of the murders was feeding information to Sheriff Maples and Deputy Davis. It is easy to see how Wynn could be arrested within days of the killings, based on the positive ID by Lizzie Chandler from the hotel window. But how about Tipton, minutes later and shortly after that, Wade, and the telegram to Asheville authorities to detain Catlett?

Somebody had to know. That was likely George Thurmer, a notorious criminal who had been pardoned while serving a term in prison for killing a Knoxville policeman. As you recall, Thurmer was indicted along with others in connection with the White Cap robbery of an old pensioner named John Burnett.

Deputy Tom Davis captured Thurmer in Knoxville sometime after the robbery, with the help of law enforcement there, and brought him back to a jail cell in Sevierville.

Thurmer was the prime instigator in the escape that included Wes Hendricks and Newt Green. Thurmer fled to Pineville, Kentucky, where he got employment helping build the foundation for a railroad trestle. His capture by Tom Davis, and return to Knoxville, was reported in the Friday, September 3, 1897, Knoxville Sentinel as follows:

"The manner in which Deputy Davis captured his man and then brought him to Tennessee without requisition papers, is worthy of mention.

"Davis on learning the whereabouts of Thurmer, got ex-Policeman Wm. Thompson to accompany him, because he knew Thurmer would recognize him (Davis.). Thompson told Thurmer, who was sailing under the alias Charles Wilson, that a man wished to speak to him a few feet distant. Not suspecting anything, he accompanied Thompson to where Davis was awaiting, whereupon he was placed under arrest by Davis whom he at once recognized. He at first flatly refused to accompany the officer to Tennessee without requisition papers, but was met with the declaration of Davis that he would be taken anyway. He then wilted and was quite willing to accompany the officer. The arrest reflects credition the abilities of Deputy Davis."[144]

It was reported on October 9, 1897, that George Thurmer was shot in the chest with a pistol by Dan Moriarty in Knoxville, in a dispute over a woman[145]. Thurmer's wound was expected to be fatal, though he recovered and moved back to Sevierville. There was some speculation that White Caps "had a hand in Thurmer's shooting, but the report is generally discredited."[146]

But back in Sevierville, Thurmer, it is surmised, began to feed intelligence about White Cap activities to the sheriff's office.

Pleas Wynn was allegedly having trouble keeping his mouth shut after the Whaley murders, and possibly the details about who all was involved in the case—both killers and co-conspirators—found their way to

---

[144] THURMER CAPTURED, *Knoxville Sentinel*, September 3, 1897
[145] MEETS HIS FATE, The Knoxville Tribune, October 9, 1897
[146] THURMER LIVES, Knoxville Tribune, October 10, 1897

Thurmer. If he learned from his contacts immediately after the Whaley murders who the perpetrators were, he may have conveyed that to the "good fellow" Davis, facilitating the rapid arrests of Tipton, Catlett and Wade so soon after the identification of Wynn.

Irrespective of who was informing on the White Caps and providing law enforcement with information on the Whaley murders, Bob Wade's case was nolle prossed, and it is unknown how his relationship with Bob Catlett was faring after Wynn and Tipton were hanged. What is known is that Catlett would have been preoccupied with keeping a noose off his own prosperous neck, and probably not interested in any activity that could compromise his defense.

Bob Wade preceded his brother-in-law in death by nearly 20 years, dying on February 28, 1921, just short of his 49th birthday.

Millard Fillmore Maples was approaching the end of his 4 years as High Sheriff of Sevier County when he gut-shot an inebriated William Wynn during the trial of Wynn's brother, Pleas, for the death of Bill Whaley. Judge T. A. R. Nelson, Jr. had Maples arrested in the shooting, and the sheriff was ultimately indicted in Wynn's death.

Maples claimed the shooting was a case of self-defense because Wynn, who Maples was attempting to take into custody and who had a group of supporters behind him, was trying to grab the sheriff's gun and turn it on him. Maples said he had to do what he did.

At trial, Maples was acquitted on September 7, 1899.

WAS ACQUITTED OF THE CHARGE

Ex-Sheriff Maples of Sevier Is a Free Man.

Verdict in the Case Rendered On Thursday.

After leaving public office, Maples migrated to Knoxville, where he worked as a deputy U.S. Marshal, a gauger for the Internal Revenue Service and a police officer. Eventually he became a bouncer and bartender at Lay's Marble City Saloon, owned by James P. Lay at 135 Central Ave. in Knoxville. Maples briefly ran his own Knoxville establishment called the Arcade Saloon, but it went out of business.

Maples bought some property in Sevier County and was planning to relocate back there when he went to visit Lay at the saloon on April 4, 1907. Some kind of disagreement developed between the men, which erupted into a full-on argument. Lay fired five shots, killing Maples almost instantly. Lay was charged with murder, but those charges were dismissed eight days later on Lay's claim of self-defense.

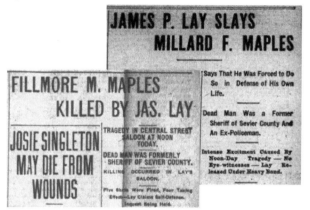

Maples was buried in Red Bank Cemetery in Sevier County. Maples' daughter, the lovely Lillie—the paramour of Dr. J.A. Henderson and the reason for his assassination—died at age 82 on December 12, 1955, in Sevier County. She and Bill Gass, who was acquitted of Henderson's murder, had three children.

John and Lizzie Chandler reconciled and resumed their life together. Lizzie died at 64 in 1937 and John, 10 years later at 75. They are buried together in Mount Carmel Cemetery in Bradley County.

Beyond her cause of death and death on August 4, 1893, not much is known about Mary Elizabeth Breeden or that of her husband, Andrew, who preceded her in death. The family's financial circumstances may have prevented the purchase of a cemetery plot for the White Cap victim, so she and her husband could simply be interred on a family farm somewhere. No death certificate for her has been found for either Mary or Andrew Breeden.

Jesse Breeden, the grown son who was prevented at gunpoint from intervening in the beatings of two of his sisters and his mother, died June 22, 1942, in Nashville. He and his wife, Sallie, had three children. One of the sisters beaten, Mary, died an old maid on October 3, 1946.

Little is known about what happened to Molly Lillard Whaley after she was orphaned. Someone, "by next friend, vs. W. R. Catlett et als," filed a lawsuit on her behalf seeking "damages for the killing of her father and mother, by Wynne and Tipton with the aid of Catlett, in December 1896."[147] The "Defendant demurred on the ground that the suit was barred by the statute of limitations of one year," and the "lower judgment sustaining demurrer was affirmed."

The following poem written about her appeared in the Crozier book, with no mention of who wrote the poem:

My name is Molly Lillard Whaley,
I'm left alone in this wide world;
Papa and mamma are dead, you know,
And I am their only baby girl.

The story is told in this little book,
Of how and why I was left alone,
How papa and mamma died one night,
In our own little cabin home.

---

[147] *Knoxville Sentinel*, October 18, 1899

How mamma pled for her own dear life ,
And for the life of dear papa, as well,
How she pressed me to her aching heart,
As she kissed me a last farewell.

She held me in her arms for a moment,
And then laid me in Aunt Lizzie's bed,
And the last words she spoke on earth
Were, "Sister, cover up your head."

Then she turned and faced the murderers,
Who stood waiting upon the floor;
Two shots rang out in quick succession,
And papa and mamma were then no more.

A deathly silence came o'er the weird scene,
Aunt Lizzie will never forget the time,
I was made fatherless, motherless and homeless,
By the commission of that awful crime.

They tell me of a fearless officer ,
Who ran those criminals down
They made him sheriff of the county,
And his name is now renowned.

They tell me of two detectives,
Who lent a helping hand
To uncover the crimes of criminals,
And break up the White- cap band.

They tell me of the Attorney General
Who made such a gallant fight
To convict those hellish demons,
Because it was just and right.

They tell me of an honorable Judge,

Who now holds court in Sevier,
Of that roving band of White- caps,
They say he has no fear.

They also tell me of another Judge,
Who sits upon a higher throne,
And if I but do his bidding,
He will one day call me home.

They say he is kind to little children,
And will guide these tiny feet,
And deal out justice to the murderers
In the death they are doomed to meet .

The Ghost of the White Caps

The debate about when Whitecapping actually ended continued well into the Twentieth Century, and some folks question whether or not it has actually ended.

In 1963, Sevier County native Marion R. Mangrum republished the Crozier book under the name, *Interment of the White Caps*, and wrote:

"After almost three-quarters of a century, ... we still have the remnants of the White Caps hovering over us like a ghost, or curse. The effect of this condition is much like epidemic disease. Those who know they have it—don't know how to get rid of it. Others scatter it not realizing the adverse effects.

Newcomers to this area [Sevier County] settle in new homes knowing nothing of the local customs. They expect to love and be loved. Suddenly there is an inexplicable barrier between the newcomer and the old Sevier County resident. Upon checking these misunderstandings we discover many have been frightened by such stories as: "you'll end up getting whipped," or, "you had better be careful—you'll get burned out," and in the higher locations a good one is, "check your brake rods before you start down the mountain," etc. A little fright, even as a prank, is extremely dangerous. Many times the ghost of the White Caps has spoiled what could have been good relationships between neighbors.[148]

We asked you to consider these questions as you read *At the Dead Hours of Midnight: A Bloody Reign of Terror in the Great Smoky Mountains*:

What was the true motivation for the proliferation of Whitecapping in Sevier County, if the estimates are correct and there were between 650-1500 White Caps conducting more than a dozen White Cap raids a night as E. W. Crozier suggests?

And if there were that many White Caps conducting that many raids, why were only a handful charged and convicted of their crimes?

Is it possible that "the powers that be" were relieved that two would pay the ultimate penalty for the sins of many, so that the Whitecapping stain would just go away?

We don't know the answers, but we believe we have presented evidence that presents a clearer picture of why Sevier County was ruled by prominent and wealthy landowners, and why there were little consequences for their having done so.

---

[148] Marion Mangrum, *Interment of the White Caps*, (Maryville, TN: Brazos Press, 1963), pp. vii - viii

ACKNOWLEDGEMENTS

Most of the heavy lifting had already been done by the time Richard and Stan agreed to work on this project, and the names of most of those contributors were acknowledged in *The Eyes of Midnight*. We are indebted to Robert "Bob" Wilson for laying the foundation for *At the Dead Hours of Midnight: A Bloody Reign of Terror in the Great Smoky Mountains* with *The Eyes of Midnight: A Time of Terror in East Tennessee*.

Kyle Perkins, of RoseWood Virtual Tours, was instrumental in capturing images of documents in the Donald F. Paine Collection in the Special Collections Department at The University of Tennessee's Hodges Library. Kyle Hovious, a Digital Specialist in the aforementioned department, was very patient and very helpful with my multiple requests, and during my many visits. Lisa Misosky, owner of Southland Books & Café in Maryville, suggested we take a look at the Peter H. Prince Collection in the Special Collections Department, and this is where we discovered the previously unpublished photographs of Laura McMahan Whaley and her sister, Lizzie McMahan Chandler.

Mae Stamey Owenby is a highly accomplished educator born in Emert's Cove in 1935, and the great-granddaughter of John Sam Springs. Mae began her teaching career in Sevier County, then moved to Blount County after her marriage. A lifelong Democrat, she is the only woman ever elected Superintendent of Blount County Schools, and was also elected to serve in the Tennessee House of Representatives, representing Blount County and part of Sevier County. Mae was very generous in sharing information about her great-grandfather, and she arranged a visit to his homestead for Richard and Debbie Way, and Stan. Thanks to Mark Stamey for providing the original picture of John Springs getting a haircut.

The John Springs Homestead in Emert's Cove has been owned by three families: John Springs, Anse and Vary Ramsey, and the Ingle family since 1956. Dr. Robert V. Ingle, DDS, and Patti Clevenger gave us the tour of the home and the grounds and extended the highest level of hospitality. While previously stated that the burial place of John Sam Springs was unknown, Mae and Vince are certain his final resting place is on property across the road from the homeplace. Chris and Erin Davenport took pictures of the Springs' homeplace, and introduced us to Vince and Patti.

There have been two gentlemen whose contributions are worth noting again. Carroll McMahan, Sevier County Historian, was even more helpful than in the original work, as he again provided some background and photographs. His foreword captures the essence of *At the Dead Hours of Midnight*, and how it differs from previous works.

Tim Fisher, Genealogist at the King Family Library in Sevierville once again provided invaluable assistance.

Acknowledgements—*The Eyes of Midnight*

On some level, *The Eyes of Midnight* can be characterized as a work of history, in that it profiles real events, real people and a real period in the life of one Tennessee county.

But in another sense, it is no more than a collection of data from multiple sources, independent of each other both in who compiled the information and the time in which they did so. This book stands astride all of those sources and benefits from research, recollection and data mining done by those who preceded it. It could not have been completed in any other fashion, and I am grateful to those who plowed this field before me to bring buried facts to the surface.

Ethelred W. Crozier was publisher of Knoxville's City Directory in the days when a book listing the city's phone numbers would have been a truly thin volume. But any pre-Internet print journalist will tell you that the City Directory in any municipality was considered a reliable cross-reference for names, addresses and—eventually—phone numbers.

Crozier's book, *The White Caps—A History of the Organization in Sevier County*, is actually erroneous on its title page. It was not a history, but a *real-time account* of the period when the White Caps wielded power in the county virtually without fear of opposition. The book was published in 1899, after Pleas Wynn and J. C. Tipton were convicted of the murders of Bill and Laura Whaley, but before they were hanged later that year. *The White Caps* identifies Crozier as publisher of the book, but no author is listed. That is likely because there were still enough feelings of betrayal, anxiety and fear of prosecution then that anyone who admitted to having penned the accounts in Crozier's book might well have become another White Cap victim.

Reading *The White Caps* 115 years later, it is not much of a stretch to conclude that Crozier himself wrote the book Crozier, who had ready access to typesetting and printing presses, had the capability to turn out a book of this nature in such a short period of time as to rival the self-publishing of a book in today's world. It is entirely possible that Crozier's book was based on actual verbal accounts by Sheriff Tom Davis. The details about many of the episodes recounted in the book would have been known only to Davis. But the effusive glorification of Davis as the singular savior of a corrupt county is probably not something the Sheriff would have written about himself.

Presumably to offset the cost of publishing *The White Caps*, Crozier accepted four display advertisements on the final pages, two from farm equipment dealers, one from a hotel and one from a candy store, all in Knoxville.

In researching *The Eyes of Midnight*, I came across a handful of statements in Crozier's book that just did not dovetail with other data, such as death certificates, census records and other records. In such cases, I fell back on my journalistic training to make a judgment call on which information would logically seem more plausible and reliable. For instance, if Crozier spelled a name one way but that person's gravestone showed it differently, I went with the grave marker, assuming that Davis's memory or attention to spelling accuracy, though sound for the most part, were more likely to be mistaken than the actions of a craftsmen being paid by the family of the deceased to get it right for all time.

Most of these discrepancies surfaced as I search an Internet genealogy database for principal characters in the White Cap saga. The search sometimes—but not always—yielded images of census rolls or other documents that also contained spellings of names or ages that were suspect. Those I reconciled the best I could.

Crozier's book also was the basis for another book published in the 1930s by the locally fabled grocer and politician Cas Walker, about whose veracity and reliability one can obtain varying opinions. Walker's book, *The White Caps of Sevier County*, reprinted swaths of Crozier's book and interspersed between them accounts presumably handed down to him by his father, Tom Walker, a known Blue Bill.

The Blue Bills, though integral to the overall chronicle of the White Cap era, were able to thwart isolated White Cap attacks. But the Blue Bills were never able to derail their opponents' activities in any significant way beyond that, and they became pretty much ineffective after their ostensible leader, Dr. J.A. Henderson was gunned down in his living room by Lillie Maples' jealous husband.

Cas Walker's book—like Crozier's, a first-generation account—probably gives the Blue Bills a higher profile in the era than they merit. And though one can speculate about Walker's motivation, he took that information with him to eternity.

There are three other information sources that deserve credit in this book. One of those is Donald Franklin Paine, a distinguished Knoxville attorney, lecturer and author, and a man apparently obsessed with accuracy, integrity and detail. He was a founding partner of the Paine, Tarwater, & Bickers law firm.

Paine undertook extensive research into the White Cap era, mostly as it pertained to the legalities involved. Paine's work unearthed court transcripts, newspaper clippings and much more from various archives and the fruits of his endeavors are catalogued at the University of Tennessee's Hodges Library. Paine died in 2013.

Of incalculable service to the writing of *The Eyes of Midnight* was Carroll McMahan, the county historian of Sevier County, who has also written on and researched the White Cap era. McMahan's institutional knowledge of the county and its background and residents was my literary GPS, steering me in the right direction whenever I asked and not doing so in one of those halting, annoying electronic voices. He can also trace his lineage back to both Aaron McMahan and Laura McMahan Whaley.

Thanks also goes to Tim Fisher, a genealogist at Sevierville's King Family Library. His knowledge of county geography and family background was as valuable as his cataloguing of others' research into the White Caps for people like me to delve into.

The Sevier County Courthouse that was funded by the county government during the era of the White Caps is still in use, though it has been modified and added onto over the decades and now has a bronze statue of Dolly Parton on the lawn. But it is no longer subject to periodic flooding as it was then, because in 1967, the Little Pigeon River, which ran just behind the courthouse and in which Pleas Wynn was baptized, was rerouted some distance away.

APPENDIX I—TIMELINE OF SIGNIFICANT WHITECAPPING EVENTS

1886-1890..............Elkanah M. Wynn, High Sheriff of Sevier County

1890-1894..............George DeLozier, High Sheriff of Sevier County

1894-1898..............Millard Fillmore Maples, High Sheriff of Sevier County

1898-1900..................Thomas Houston Davis, High Sheriff of Sevier County

January 27, 1892....White Caps of Emert's Cove first mentioned in a newspaper article

May 18, 1892..........First mention of Blue Bills in a newspaper article

April 25, 1892.....…......…......Russell Jenkins beaten by White Caps

July 14, 1892.........…..........Eli Williamson murdered by White Caps

May 1893.........................Breeden women beaten by White Caps

August 4, 1893.................Mary Breeden died as a result of beating

April 29, 1894...............Bruce Llewellyn murdered by White Caps?

September 22, 1894.........White Cap Riot at Congressman Houk Speech in Gatlinburg

October 25, 1894...........................Battle of Henderson Springs

November 30, 1894......Dr. James A. Henderson murdered by William "Bill" Gass

January 2, 1895..............Sallie Deats shot and killed by Sam Jenkins

April 27, 1895....................Tom Gibson murdered by White Caps

July 15, 1896................Aaron McGill (McMahan), Amos McGill and James Clabough ambushed by Green and Hendricks

November 1896..................................Andrew Henderson robbed

November 1896................Bob Catlett and Bob Wade indicted for rocking and shooting Walter Maples' home

December 28, 1896......................Bill and Laura Whaley Murdered

January 4, 1897................Lizzie Chandler identifies Pleasant Wynn; Wynn and Tipton, Catlett and Wade arrested

January 4, 1897................Tipton and Wynn brought before Justice of the Peace and released pending Grand Jury action

January 5, 1897...................................Bob Wade surrendered

January 16, 1897.........Catlett and Wade brought before a Justice of the Peace; Catlett released on bond, Wade remained in jail

March 1897...................Wes Hendrick and Newt Green convicted of murdering Aaron McGill

March 24, 1897...............................anti-White Cap Law enacted

July 1897 ....Sevier County placed under jurisdiction of Judge T. A. R. Nelson, Jr.

November 15-26, 1897...............Trial I of Tipton and Wynn for murder of Laura Whaley; Wynn convicted; Tipton acquitted

April 5-8, 1898....Trial II of Tipton and Wynn for murder of William Whaley; both convicted, both sentenced to hang

April 6, 1898.........Sheriff Millard Fillmore Maples shot William Wynn

November 18, 1898................State Supreme Court affirmed convictions and death sentences of Tipton and Wynn

February 6-11, 1899....Trial I of Bob Catlett in Hamblen County for procuring the murder of William Whaley—mistrial

May 1899.........Trial II of Bob Catlett in Hamblen County for procuring the murder of William Whaley—acquitted and escaped

May 1899......Bob Catlett Escapes Re-Arrest; surrenders in November 1901

July 5, 1899.........James Catlett Tipton and Pleasant D. Wynn Hanged

February 1903.....Trial III of Bob Catlett in Loudon County for procuring the murder of Laura Whaley—mistrial

June 8-13, 1903...Trial IV of Bob Catlett in Loudon County for procuring the murder of Laura Whaley—convicted and sentenced to hang

October 31, 1903...Bob Catlett Case Reversed by the Tennessee State Supreme Court

April 4-9, 1904......Trial V of Bob Catlett for procuring the murder of Laura Whaley

April 9, 1904....................Bob Catlett Acquitted on second ballot

Index

A

About the Authors

Richard Way, Lieutenant Colonel, United States Air Force, Retired, is a retired commercial airline pilot and entrepreneur from Knoxville, Tennessee. He graduated from the University of Tennessee in 1968, and was commissioned through the R.O.T.C. program. He went on to graduate from the Undergraduate Pilot Training at Laredo Air Force Base in Laredo, Texas. He served in the United States Air Force and Tennessee Air National Guard for a combined twenty-three years. His decorations include the Distinguished Flying Cross, Meritorious Service Medal and Air Medal. He and his wife Debbie have three children, and four grandchildren.

He commissioned *The Eyes of Midnight: A Time of Terror in East Tennessee*, which was published in 2016. He also published a collection of military aircraft photographs, *A Young Tiger's Tale*, taken during his time in the United States Air Force and Tennessee Air National Guard.

Stanford Johnson is an East Tennessee native and member of First Families of Tennessee. A two-time honorably discharged and former homeless Army Veteran, he served as an enlisted Military Policeman in Berlin from January 1984 to December 1986. He completed his commissioning requirements in R.O.T.C. and degree requirements at The University of North Georgia, in June 1990, then served as a battery-level field artillery officer from August 1990 to April 1994. His decorations include the Army Commendation Medal, the Army Achievement Medal with Oak Leaf Cluster, the Army of Occupation Medal, the Army Good Conduct Medal and the National Defense Service Medal.

He published a novel, *Our LITTLE Secret: A Smoky Mountains Family Saga and Coming of Age Story Inspired by True Crimes* in 2021, and was the editor for *A Young Tiger's Tale*, a collection of military aircraft photographs taken by Lieutenant Colonel Richard Way, USAF, Retired, in 2022.

Made in the USA
Columbia, SC
04 May 2025

57510149R00141